THE SECOND STEPHEN KING QUIZ BOOK

Stephen Spignesi

A SIGNET BOOK

SIGNET
Published by the Penguin Group
Penguin Books USA Inc., 375 Hudson Street,
New York, New York 10014, U.S.A.
Penguin Books Ltd, 27 Wrights Lane,
London W8 5TZ, England
Penguin Books Australia Ltd, Ringwood,
Victoria, Australia
Penguin Books Canada Ltd, 10 Alcorn Avenue,
Toronto, Ontario, Canada M4V 3B2
Penguin Books (N.Z.) Ltd, 182–190 Wairau Road,
Auckland 10, New Zealand

Penguin Books Ltd, Registered Offices:
Harmondsworth, Middlesex, England

First published by Signet, an imprint of New American Library,
a division of Penguin Books USA Inc.

First Printing, July, 1992
10 9 8 7 6 5 4 3 2 1

 REGISTERED TRADEMARK—MARCA REGISTRADA

PRINTED IN THE UNITED STATES OF AMERICA

TERROR-IFIC TRIVIA PURSUIT

What did the Losers use as bullets
when they shot It?

Who was on Kurt Dussander's List of Great
Murderers from the Past?

Getting It On was the original title
for which King book?

In the movie *Graveyard Shift,* what was the name
of the mill that kept Gates Falls alive and who
was it named for? (Warning: Trick Question!)

THE SECOND STEPHEN KING QUIZ BOOK

STEPHEN SPIGNESI is the author of *The Stephen King Quiz Book*, *The Shape Under the Sheet: The Complete Stephen King Encyclopedia*, and *Mayberry, My Hometown*, a highly regarded look at the *Andy Griffith Show*. He is married and lives in New Haven, Connecticut.

This book is for
my aunt Marge and uncle Steve Rapuano
with love and gratitude;

and also for my brothers and sister,
Paul, David, and Janet.

"I was born . . . of a good family . . ."
—DANIEL DEFOE

Contents

Booze, Beasts, Dates, Mates, Kodes, Kritics, Rhymes, & Rods   137

INTRODUCTION

"A Mind Clapping"

"I can say little more than I have studied,
and that question's out of my part."
　　　　—William Shakespeare, from *Twelfth Night*

What *is* the answer? . . . In that case, what is the
question?
　　　　—The last words of Gertrude Stein

The first time I saw Mike Nichols's film *Postcards
From the Edge* (starring Meryl Streep and Shirley
MacLaine), I actually applauded three times during
the run of the film—but I wasn't in a theater.

I was watching the movie on video at home, alone
in my office, and I actually found myself clapping
three separate times during the film, so delighted was
I by the excellence of the writing, the performances,
the directing, or the cinematic moment. (Mike Nichols, for my money, is one of the best American directors ever. His credits include the aforementioned
Postcards, as well as *Carnal Knowledge, Catch-22, The
Graduate, Heartburn, Silkwood* (both also with Meryl
Streep), *Biloxi Blues, Who's Afraid of Virginia
Woolf?, Gilda Live,* and the ever-optimistic and uplift-
ing *Working Girl*. His body of work is interesting,
enjoyable, and masterfully directed.)

This, I thought to myself, is what artistic achieve-
ment is all about.

I won't pinpoint the specific scenes that elicited such a response from me (although Shirley MacLaine's rendering of Stephen Sondheim's "I'm Still Here" [in D flat] and Meryl Streep's acting are definitely in my Top Ten): I'll leave it to you to decide for yourself which particular moments work for you. But the point is that only excellence in *the arts* is capable of mustering such an emotional reaction. We don't find ourselves wanting to give a standing ovation to a brilliantly executed spreadsheet. (Unless you're a somewhat fixated CPA, that is!) Nor do we ever have an urge to yell "Bravo!" after having some successful minor surgery done. (*That* would make the recovery room a rather lively place, eh?!)

But art has a power that transcends; that elevates; that inspires; that *moves*.

There have been other artistic works—works that are intrinsically and genuinely *excellent*—that have triggered such a reaction from me.

A handful of them include:

- The Ivan Neville song "Why Can't I Fall in Love?" and the Leonard Cohen/Concrete Blonde tune "Everybody Knows" (for its brilliant lyrics), both from the *Pump Up the Volume* soundtrack;
- Don Dorsey's synthesized version of the "Presto" section of Bach's *Italian Concerto* from Don's *Bachbusters* album;
- Just about any single "episode" of "Late Night with David Letterman";
- All of J.R.R. Tolkien's *Lord of the Rings* trilogy;
- The song "The Way You Look Tonight" by Jerome Kern and Dorothy Fields;
- Woody Allen's films *Manhattan, Hannah and Her Sisters,* and *Crimes and Misdemeanors*, as well as his performance as Danny Rose in his own film *Broadway Danny Rose*;
- Mia Farrow's amazing performance as a seductive temptress in Woody's film *Alice* (speaking of the Woodman);

- Kate Bush's songs "Running Up That Hill," "And Dream of Sheep," and "Under Ice" from her incredible *Hounds of Love* album;
- George Gershwin's "Rhapsody in Blue";
- Ellen Goodman's and Joan Didion's essays;
- Richard Dworsky's Windham Hill solo piano composition "A Morning With The Roses";
- Dick Allen's poems "Autumn Lightning" and "The People Through the Train Window" from his poetry collection *Overnight in the Guest House of the Mystic*;
- All of Marvin Hamlisch's *A Chorus Line* score;
- Any episode of "The Andy Griffith Show," "All in the Family," or "M*A*S*H";
- Any short story by J. D. Salinger;
- The Bob Dylan song "Like a Rolling Stone";
- Any of Robin Williams's stand-up work;
- The magnificent limited editions published by Donald M. Grant;
- Anything by the Beatles (especially the *White Album*, but not their versions of stuff they didn't write);
- Any painting by Salvador Dali or Edward Hopper;
- Pauline Kael's and Roger Ebert's film reviews;
- The white broccoli pizza at Aniello's in East Haven, Connecticut (okay, pizza is not strictly a *work of art*, but let's make a certain Italian happy and pretend it is for the purposes of this discussion);
  and, of course . . .
- The work of Stephen King.

The title of this introduction, "A Mind Clapping," refers to the Zen *koan*, "What is the sound of one hand clapping?" and metaphorically alludes to the inexplicable and mysterious process the reader/viewer/listener goes through while experiencing—and reacting to—excellence in the arts.

The way *Postcards From the Edge* overwhelmed me

enough to clap out loud, so does the work of Stephen King move me enough to clap in my mind. (Reading being the quiet, introspective, personal pursuit it is, it would *really* seem weird to clap while reading a book, wouldn't it?)

But you catch my drift. As the *koan* is almost impossible to answer, so is it almost impossible to discern the process by which we recognize and identify excellence. We've all felt it, though: that involuntary urge to put your hands together in acknowledgment of *something supreme*—even if those two hands *are* holding a book.

King's work has achieved levels of excellence over the years that have won him incalculable millions of fans, and made him one of the most popular American authors and performing artists ever to live.

Now even though the term "performing arts" is generally considered to encompass film, stage, music, and dance, I think we can take that definition one step further and designate Stephen King as a practitioner of the performing arts. ("But writers don't *perform*," I hear you objecting, "so strictly interpreted, your definition ain't gonna play, Steve.")

But I'm not thinking of Stephen King's "writing" as part of the performing arts. It *doesn't* fit in the strictest sense of the term. But if you consider his *storytelling* as an artistic performance, then it works.

Stephen King is an expert storyteller; a virtuoso; a master.

When you read a King tale, you are engaged, captivated, and enthralled.

Stephen King has a power: It is the power to make us agog.

In the summer of 1991, the British publisher Hodder & Stoughton released an "exclusive presentation proof" of two works by Stephen King: *Needful Things*, and "Secret Window, Secret Garden" from *Four Past Midnight*. The title of this dual volume was *Twice the Power*.

16

I find that well-put.

This is the second volume of *The Stephen King Quiz Book*. The first volume was published in August 1990, and covered King's works from *Carrie* through *The Dark Half*. It also included many of King's uncollected short stories.

This second volume takes up where Volume I left off, beginning with *The Stand: The Complete & Uncut Edition* and it includes *Four Past Midnight*, *Needful Things*, and *The Dark Tower III: The Waste Lands*.

All of the films released since the summer of 1990 are covered, as are King's most recent new short stories, "The Moving Finger" and "You Know They Got a Hell of a Band."

In Volume I, I had to concentrate on covering (i.e. "quizzing") all of King's works that had been published up through 1990. This required lots of basic questioning, and lots of space. Since Volume I, then, takes care of the bulk of King's work, I was able to let loose a little in Volume II and cover material I wasn't able to include in the first book.

Thus, in Volume II, you will find quizzes on songs, cigarettes, booze, and weapons. You will also find more detailed quizzes on the films, as well as quizzes on vehicles, animals, poems, and books *about* King.

And as always, because the work from which the question was drawn is given to you, it is my hope that you won't just skip over those questions to which you do not immediately know the answer, but rather return to the stories and hunt the correct answer down. That's the fun part: rereading Stephen King's stuff.

The Second Stephen King Quiz Book is in nine sections:

I. A Royal Reopening
II. Book-Length Works
III. The New Uncollected Short Stories

The Second Stephen King Quiz Book also contains an updated bibliography of the books and stories "quizzed" in this volume, as well as an updated selection of recommended books, magazines, and sources.

Since *The Stephen King Quiz Book* was released in 1990, I have also published *The Shape Under the Sheet: The Complete Stephen King Encyclopedia* (Popular Culture, Ink., 1991). *The Shape Under the Sheet* is a 750,000-word Stephen King encyclopedia which had King's cooperation and participation and which contains more than 18,000 entries of fact from Stephen King's works, divided into People, Places, and Things sections. There are also dozens of interviews, essays, articles, sidebars, photos, and illustrations of interest for the King fan. Many of the quizzes in this second quiz book will be much easier to solve if you have access to *The Shape*. See the Bibliography for more information on *The Shape Under the Sheet* and other helpful volumes.

Okay, I'll shut up now . . . but first, let me toss a few bouquets. You don't mind, do ya?

ACKNOWLEDGMENTS

My sincerest thanks and fondest appreciation goes to the following angels:

- My wife, Pam, who *also* knows why . . .
- My mother, the ever-amazing Lee;
- Elaine Koster, for granting me the privilege of doing Volume II;
- My editors Matt Sartwell and Ed Stackler, for their advice, support, good humor, and profound talents;
- Matt's assistant Peter Borland, for his friendliness, and for *always* going out of his way to help in ways too numerous to mention;
- My Popular Culture, Ink. editor, Tom Schultheiss, for his friendship, and for his continuing kindness, advice, and help—even for books he's not publishing!;
- My agent John White, for everything;
- My friend Pat Curtis, for her warmth, her sincerity, and her appreciation of Italian cooking;
- My dear friend, George Beahm, a man of words, and a man of his word;
- My pal, Louanne Deserio, for getting rid of the part, and for always listening;
- My friends and colleagues (terrific people all!): Katherine Flickinger and Linda Zmarthie, Dave Hinchberger and Laurie Hinchberger, Rick Hautala (I *do* hope you've been reading Rick since the last time we talked! He's *still* terrific!), Stanley Wiater, Michael Collings, J. N. Williamson, Tyson Blue (Stanley, Michael, J. N., and Tyson are *also* well worth your reading time, my friends), Shirley Sonderegger, Elyce Rexer, Dave Lowell, David King, Chris Chesley, Donna Martin, Jim Cole, Ted DeMaio, Judy Heaney, Gary Dermer, Mike Streeto, Linda Beavis, Moshe Bezalel, Efraim Bezalel, and Jackie.

- Frank "Franklin Pierce" Mandato, for all his help and support, and for everything he's meant to me over the years;
- My family, Ben, Paul, Laura, David, Maureen, Janet, Jerry, Amanda, Jennifer, Joey, John, Amy, Dolores, Tony, Linda, Sheryl, Vinnie, and Tomasina;
- and Stephen King . . . again.

Quizzes are meant to be fun.
You have your orders.
You may begin.

—Stephen Spignesi
December 1991
New Haven, Connecticut

I

A ROYAL REOPENING

"MORE EPIGRAPHS OF STEPHEN KING"

Quiz 1

"There must be a beginning of any great matter, but the continuing unto the end until it be thoroughly finished yields the true glory."
—Sir Francis Drake

". . . mighty things from small beginnings grow . . ."
—John Dryden, *Annus Mirabilis*

Webster's defines an epigraph as "a quotation set at the beginning of a literary work or a division of it to suggest a theme." Stephen King has long been a faithful user of epigraphs to lead off many of his works, and his selections have always added a fillip of insight to our reading. (You don't skip over them, now, *do you*? I hope not, because if you do, then this quiz is going to be a tad tough!)

Identify the Stephen King works that contain the following epigraphs as well as the author of the original quote, and the work from which the quotation was drawn.

1. "We need help, the Poet reckoned."
2. "My surface is myself.
     Under which
   to witness, youth is
     buried. Roots?

   Everybody has roots."

3. "When you look into the abyss, the abyss also looks into you."
4. "Dirty deeds done dirt cheap."
5. "I've Got No Car And It's Breaking My Heart But I've Found A Driver And That's A Start . . ."
6. "This column has
A hole. Can you see
The Queen of the Dead?"
7. "Hey-ho, let's go."
8. "And now our contestants are in the isolation booth."
9. " 'Cut him,' Machine said. 'Cut him while I stand here and watch. I want to see the blood flow. Don't make me tell you twice.' "
10. "In the desert
I saw a creature, naked, bestial,
Who, squatting upon the ground,
Held his heart in his hands,
And ate of it.

I said, 'Is it good, friend?'
'It is bitter-bitter,' he answered;
'But I like it
Because it is bitter
And because it is my heart.' "
11. "I'm your boogie man
that's what I am
and I'm here to do
whatever I can . . ."
12. "You can't be careful on a skateboard, man."
13. "Meet the new boss. Same as the old boss."
14. "Old Blue died and he died so hard
He shook the ground in my back yard.
I dug his grave with a silver spade
And I lowered him down with a golden chain.
Every link you know I did call his name,
I called, 'Here, Blue, you good dog, you.' "
15. "Come on, assholes! You want to live forever?"
16. "Well we'll really have a party but we gotta post a guard outside . . ."

17. "In the stinking darkness under the barn, he raised his shaggy head. His yellow, stupid eyes gleamed. 'I hunger,' he whispered."

18. "So you understand that when we increase the number of variables, the axioms themselves never change."

19. "Ah, love, let us be true
To one another! for the world, which seems
To lie before us like a land of dreams,
So various, so beautiful, so new,
Hath really neither joy, nor love, nor light,
Nor certitude, nor peace, nor help for pain;
And we are here as on a darkling plain
Swept with confused alarms of struggle and flight,
Where ignorant armies clash by night."

20. "We need help, the Poet reckoned."

"MORE OPENERS"

Quiz 2

This quiz once again tests your knowledge of the first lines of Stephen King's works. For each "opener," identify the work it begins. (There are an additional five "Bonus Openers" for all you *real* Stephen King experts out there! These bonus first lines are all from very rare and hard-to-find King works—but all the works *have* been published at one time or another. So give them your best shot and if you can't come up with the titles, then look at the answers, and, as always, use your newfound King erudition to amaze and impress your friends! What the hell . . . it's a cheap thrill, right?)

1. "Once upon a time, not so long ago, a monster came to the small town of Castle Rock, Maine."
2. "In the year 1927 we were playing jazz in a speakeasy just south of Morgan, Illinois, a town seventy miles from Chicago."
3. "I believe there was only one occasion upon which I actually solved a crime before my slightly fabulous friend, Mr. Sherlock Holmes."
4. "Sally."
5. "September 15th was Kevin's birthday, and he got exactly what he wanted: a Sun."
6. "The most important things are the hardest things to say."
7. "But Viet Nam was over and the country was getting on."
8. "Two A.M., Friday."
9. "People's lives—their real lives, as opposed to

their simple physical existences—begin at different times."

10. "I got Katrina's letter yesterday, less than a week after my father and I got back from Los Angeles."

11. "By the time he graduated college, John Smith had forgotten all about the bad fall he took on the ice that January day in 1953."

12. "Garish walked out of the bright May sunshine and into the coolness of the dorm."

13. " 'You stole my story,' the man on the doorstep said."

14. "I can't go out no more."

15. "It was half past five in the afternoon by the time John and Elise Graham finally found their way into the little town of Willow, Maine."

16. "The terror, which would not end for another twenty-eight years—if it ever did end—began, so far as I know or can tell, with a boat made from newspaper floating down a gutter swollen with rain."

17. "I parked the heap around the corner from Keenan's house, sat in the dark for a moment, then turned off the key and got out."

18. "There's a guy like me in every state and federal prison in America, I guess—I'm the guy who can get it for you."

19. "When Mary woke up, they were lost."

20. "An old blue Ford pulled into the guarded parking lot that morning, looking like a small, tired dog after a hard run."

Bonus Openers
(For Stephen King Experts)

21. "In Ebbets Field the crab-grass grows . . ."

22. "The house was tall, with an incredible slope of shingled roof."

23. "Wharton moved slowly up the wide steps, hat

in hand, craning his neck to get a better look at the Victorian monstrosity that his sister had died in."

24. "The old man sat in the barn doorway in the smell of apples, rocking, wanting not to want to smoke not because of the doctor but because now his heart fluttered all the time."

25. "It was October 7, 1922, and the Overlook Hotel had closed its doors on the end of another season."

II

BOOK-LENGTH
WORKS

THE STAND: THE COMPLETE & UNCUT EDITION

Quiz 3

The following questions are from *The Stand: The Complete & Uncut Edition*. These questions concern information found *only* in the revised edition of *The Stand*. For a quiz on the original version of the novel, see *The Stephen King Quiz Book*.

1. Who was "Brother Zeno"?
2. What did Eileen Drummond find in her son's bedroom after his death?
3. Who ". . . looked like Baby Elvis"?
4. Who wrote *Rimfire Christmas*?
5. What was Stu Redman's code name after he was taken into custody at the Atlanta plague facility?
6. Who told Rachel Timms "you have been using that strawberry douche again"?
7. Who originated army communique #771 about the neutralization of Brodsky?
8. Before the flu, Pop Mann owned a general store in what Nebraska town?
9. To whom did Stu Redman say, "If you are who I think you are, you're supposed to be dead," and what was the gentleman's reply?
10. How did Irma Fayette die?
11. What was the name of the Reno, Nevada, man who stepped on a rusty nail and tried to amputate his own foot when it turned gangrenous?
12. After Larry Underwood moved in with Yvonne

Wetterlen, he got a job singing with a bar band. What was the name of the band?

13. Who was Spike?
14. What was the name of Jory Baker's band?
15. Who was responsible for the Mei Lai massacre?

FOUR PAST MIDNIGHT
"The Langoliers"

Quiz 4

The following questions are from the novella "The Langoliers" from the collection *Four Past Midnight*.

1. What was the name of the British secret agent who sacrificed himself on the return trip through the rip in time so that the other survivors could live?
2. Who was "Crew-Neck"?
3. How was Albert Kaussner known from Sedalia to Steamboat Springs?
4. Where did Anne Engle live (and die)?
5. From what university did Laurel Stevenson graduate with a master's degree in library science?
6. What was the number of the computer program Brian Engle used to fly from Bangor to Los Angeles on the return trip through time?
7. Anne Engle's perfume was not Lissome, Lithsome, Lithium, Lawnboy, Lifebuoy, Lovebite, Lovelorn, or Love Boy. What was it?
8. Where was Nick Hopewell shot in the leg?
9. What was written over the airplane cabin window in Brian Engle's dream about his dead wife Anne?
10. Who played Harry in *When Harry Met Sally . . .*"?

FOUR PAST MIDNIGHT
"Secret Window, Secret Garden"

Quiz 5

The following questions are from the novella "Secret Window, Secret Garden" from the collection *Four Past Midnight*.

1. What was the name of Morton Rainey's short story originally published in the June 1980 issue of *Ellery Queen's Mystery Magazine*?
2. What was the name of the Mississippi author who claimed he wrote the short story "Secret Window, Secret Garden"?
3. Who was the author of the short story "Crowfoot Mile"?
4. Where did Mort and Amy Rainey live before their divorce?
5. What was the name of Morton Rainey's third novel?
6. What publishing company published Mort Rainey's short-story collection *Everybody Drops the Dime*?
7. What was the name of the Raineys' cat?
8. What was the name of Amy Rainey's lover?
9. What was the value of the restored Victorian owned by Mort and Amy Rainey?
10. What was the name of Mort Rainey's literary agent?

FOUR PAST MIDNIGHT
"The Library Policeman"

Quiz 6

The following questions are from the novella "The Library Policeman" from the collection *Four Past Midnight*.

1. What was the name of the circus the Amazing Joe worked for?
2. What was the name of the shape-changing Junction City librarian?
3. What kind of hat did the Library Policeman wear?
4. What Junction City street was the Angel Street Homeless Shelter on?
5. What restaurant made a terrific pepperoni-and-double-mushroom pizza?
6. What was "Dirty Dave" 's last name?
7. What was the name of the Des Moines bookstore where Sam Peebles bought replacement copies of *Best Loved Poems of the American People* and *The Speaker's Companion*?
8. Who said, "I cannot live without books"?
9. What was the favorite novel of the kids who participated in the poll taken during the Junction City summer reading program?
10. What baseball team's faces did Dirty Dave paint on baseballs for Joey Soames?

FOUR PAST MIDNIGHT
"The Sun Dog"

Quiz 7

The following questions are from the novella "The Sun Dog" from the collection *Four Past Midnight*.

1. What did Kevin Delevan get for his fifteenth birthday?
2. What was the name of Kevin's sister?
3. Who was the first man to calculate the location of Pluto?
4. Where did the Sun Dog live?
5. What was the name of Pop Merrill's antique/junk shop?
6. Ace Merrill was serving four years in Shawshank Prison for breaking into what Castle Rock bar?
7. How much did John Delevan bet on the Boston Celtics–Philadelphia Seventy-Sixers game?
8. What happened in the Tecumseh House?
9. What was Aunt Hilda's annual birthday gift to Kevin?
10. What was Kevin Delevan's sixteenth birthday present?

NEEDFUL THINGS

Quiz 8

Needful Things, the "last Castle Rock story," is a masterful story told in a leisurely manner reminiscent at times of both Ray Bradbury and Thornton Wilder. (How's that for a lineage?!)

Fans of Stephen King will perhaps be dismayed to learn that *Needful Things* will probably be the last time we visit Castle Rock, Maine. But all good things must come to an end, and at least Stephen King was kind enough to allow us to watch the Rock go out with a bang!

This quiz consists of thirty *"Needful Things"* questions, broken into "People," "Places," and "Things" sections.

People

1. What was the name of Brian Rusk's speech therapist?
2. What was the name of Brian Rusk's kid brother?
3. What was the name of Sally Ratcliffe's fiancé?
4. Who was Castle Rock's Head Selectman?
5. What was the name of Nettie Cobb's dog?
6. What was the name of the Mellow Tiger's owner and bartender?
7. What nickname did John LaPointe, Seat Thomas, and Andy Clutterbuck call Norris Ridgewick?
8. What was the name of Polly Chalmers's doctor?
9. What was the name of the principal of the Castle Rock Middle School?

10. What was the name of the Jerzycks's next-door neighbors?

Places

1. What was the name of the Castle Rock Catholic Church?
2. What business was in the building Needful Things occupied prior to their moving in?
3. Where did Leland Gaunt tell people he was from?
4. Where did Wilma Jerzyck work?
5. Where did Sheriff Pangborn's son Al go to school?
6. At what Castle Rock intersection did Wilma Jerzyck and Nettie Cobb "settle their feud"?
7. Where were Albert Gendron's dental offices?
8. Where did the cocaine Mr. Gaunt gave Ace Merrill come from, and what other King book also mentions this place?
9. Where was Mr. Gaunt's Tucker garaged?
10. Where was the new store called Answered Prayers scheduled to open?

Things

1. What was the date of the Needful Things grand opening?
2. On his first visit to Needful Things, what did Brian Rusk buy from Mr. Gaunt?
3. What medication did Polly Chalmers take when her arthritis pain was particularly bad?
4. What stress-relieving diversion did Sheriff Pangborn indulge in after (or even sometimes during) particularly trying meetings or times?
5. What was the "deed" Leland Gaunt had Brian do as part of the payment for his "purchase" at Needful Things?
6. What brand of fishing rod did Norris Ridgewick

consider to be "the best damned lake-and-stream fishing rod in the world"?

7. What were the two rules of Wilma Jerzyck's confrontational life-style?

8. What was the pendant Mr. Gaunt sold Polly Chalmers for her arthritis called?

9. What was the name of the "horse-player's Ouija board" game Mr. Gaunt sold to Buster Keeton?

10. According to Sheriff Pangborn, what were the only three valid purposes microwaves served?

THE DARK TOWER III: THE WASTE LANDS

Quiz 9

"And I will show you something different from either
Your shadow at morning striding behind you,
Or your shadow at evening rising to meet you
I will show you fear in a handful of dust."
—T. S. Eliot, from *The Waste Land*

"Find other lands beneath another sun."
—James Thomson, from *The Seasons*, "Autumn"

The Dark Tower III: The Waste Lands is the third volume of Stephen King's *Dark Tower* series.

This series contains some of the most inspired and imaginative writing King has ever done. One gets the sense that the storytelling possibilities available to King within the series are boundless: the creative and amazing characters, scenarios, and situations in the tale leave one awestruck and entranced.

A friend of mine, a well-known nonfiction writer working within the field, said that he gets the feeling that because King is essentially working within a genre of his own design (you know, the "fantasy/western/ science fiction/quest/horror" genre), he is not limited by what he would reasonably be able to get away with in any *one* of those individual genres. My friend has a point. King seems more willing to wield his formidable imaginative powers in the *Dark Tower* series than he might in, say, a novel like *Misery*, or even *The Dark Half*, for instance.

I guess you could say King gets to go nuts with the *Tower* series.

In his "Author's Note" afterword to *The Waste Lands*, King tells us that even though some of us may feel that he ended this "chapter" somewhat abruptly, he knew that if he continued past the point where the story "wrote itself," the tale would be forced. So he decided to stop where serendipity told him to. This is admirable, intelligent, and correct. And it is also the sign of the consummate storyteller. King knows that the stories *must* write themselves, and he is wise enough to stop writing when that "inner storyteller" tells him to. But he assures us ("assuming the continuation of Constant Writer's life and Constant Reader's interest") that the fourth volume of the *Dark Tower* series should appear relatively soon.

In the meantime, we have more of Roland's story to ponder.

The following quiz is broken into three sections, "People," "Places," and "Things." There's a total of forty-five questions: fifteen "People," ten "Places," and twenty "Things." There is also one "Bonus Question" that cannot be answered with words.

People

1. Which of the Twelve Guardians held the earth on his shell, and on whose back all vows were made?
2. What was the name of Jake's father?
3. What was the name of Jake's French teacher?
4. What was the name of the secretary of Jake's school?
5. Who was the headmaster of Jake's school?
6. What was the name of Jake's English Group teacher?
7. Who wrote and illustrated *Charlie the Choo-Choo*?
8. What was the name of the guy who sold Jake *Charlie the Choo-Choo*?

41

9. Who did Jake see playing basketball in the dream he had before he left on his quest?
10. What was the name of the old woman matriarch in River Crossing?
11. What was the name of the warrior-prince who led the last band of outlaws that attacked Lud?
12. Who did Roland and company meet at the Lud side of the bridge?
13. Who was the last to go nigh Blaine?
14. What was the name of Roland's grandmother?
15. What was the Tick-Tock Man's real name?

Places

1. What was the original name of the forest where the Bear lived?
2. What was the name of the company that manufactured Shardik?
3. What was the name of the bottomless crack in the earth that gave off a great burst of steam every thirty or forty days?
4. What was the Great Portal, or the Thirteenth Gate?
5. What was the Victorian wreck in Dutch Hill known as?
6. Where was Tom and Gerry's Artistic Deli located?
7. Where did Jake buy *Charlie the Choo-Choo*?
8. What happened to the Mansion during Jake's crossover to Mid-World?
9. What direction of travel was Blaine responsible for?
10. What was Blaine's southeastern route?

Things

1. How did gunslingers shoot?
2. What did "Mir" mean to the Old People?
3. What was Shardik's serial number?

4. What did Hax say was the last act of the Great Old Ones?

5. What two things did Walter's jawbone transform into when Roland threw it in the fire?

6. What did *ka-tet* mean?

7. What was the name of the forces that bound space, size, and dimension together in proper alignment?

8. Match the cooking style with the author:
   1. Hard-Boiled   A. William Faulkner
   2. Fresh-Boiled   B. Raymond Chandler
   3. Pan-Fried   C. John D. MacDonald

9. What did Jake find in the vacant lot?

10. What can run but never walks,
    Has a mouth but never talks,
    Has a bed but never sleeps,
    Has a head but never weeps?

11. How far was it to Lud from River Crossing?

12. What was *graf*?

13. Who did "Velcro Fly"?

14. What was the name of Jake's billy-bumbler?

15. What was Eddie's mother's favorite saying?

16. In the old tongue, what did *char* mean?

17. While chasing Gasher and Jake, what booby-trap did Roland trigger by throwing a piece of concrete at a cobblestone?

18. What was Tick-Tock Man's password on the day Gasher brought back Jake?

19. "There is a thing that nothing is, And yet it has a name; 'tis sometimes tall and sometimes short; It joins our talks, it joins our sport, and plays at every game." What is it?

20. What was the axle upon which Roland's *ka* revolved?

Bonus Question

21. What was the code that primed Blaine's pump backwards?

III

THE NEW UNCOLLECTED SHORT STORIES

"THE MOVING FINGER"

Quiz 10

"The Moving Finger writes; and, having writ,
Moves on . . ."

Edward Fitzgerald
The Rubáiyát of Omar Khayyám (1859)

"The Moving Finger" appeared in a special "Stephen King" issue of *Fantasy & Science Fiction* magazine in December of 1990. As I said in *The Shape Under the Sheet*, "The Moving Finger" is notable for a couple of reasons: first, it adds another story to King's use of the "Bathroom Motif" (along with *It* and "Sneakers"), and second, it is hilarious. Darkly hilarious, but funny nonetheless. If you thought *Heathers* was a riot, and if *Twin Peaks* made you laugh as often as cringe, then "The Moving Finger" will be right up your alley.

The King issue of *Fantasy & Science Fiction* is still readily available at cover price from all the usual dealers, as well as direct from the publisher. (If you don't own this issue, you should. The magazine also contained the opening segment from the third *Dark Tower* book, *The Waste Lands*.)

1. What was the name of Howard Mitla's wife?
2. What did Howard do for a living?
3. Who called the cops on Howard during his battle with the finger?
4. Who is the host of *Jeopardy*?
5. What was the name of the beer on sale that Howard's wife bought?

6. Where did the Mitlas live?
7. What did Howard do in order to distract his "bashful bladder" while trying to urinate?
8. "This group of hippies crossed the United States in a bus with writer Ken Kesey."
9. What sound did the moving finger make?
10. "Why do terrible things like cancer and murder and fingers in the drain happen to the nicest people?"

"You Know They Got a Hell of a Band"

Quiz 11

"Poppa-ooo-mow-mow"

"You Know They Got a Hell of a Band" is a new Stephen King short story that made its first appearance in a 1992 Pocket Books anthology edited by Jeff Gelb, called *Shock Rock: The New Sound of Horror*.

The story, inspired by the old Righteous Brothers song "Rock and Roll Heaven," answers the question, where *do* old rockers go when they die?, and more important, do they keep on keepin' on?

We find out the answers to these questions . . . and more, in "You Know They Got a Hell of a Band." (Feed your head.)

1. Where did Mary and Clark Willingham live?
2. What kind of work did Clark do?
3. What was Mary's idea of a vacation?
4. Who sang "Six Days on the Road"?
5. What kind of car did Mary and Clark own?
6. What was the car's name?
7. Who sang "Busload of Faith"?
8. What was the name of the Pennsylvania town from which Ralph Ginzburg once tried to mail his magazine *Eros*?
9. How did the town limits "welcome" sign describe Rock and Roll Heaven, Oregon?

10. What was the name of the Rock and Roll Heaven barber shop?
11. What was the name of the Rock and Roll Heaven pharmacy?
12. What was the name of the Rock and Roll Heaven pet shop?
13. What was the name of the Rock and Roll Heaven diner?
14. What singer was one of the waitresses at the town diner?
15. What was the diner hot dog called?
16. What was the diner cheeseburger called?
17. What was the diner quarter-pound cheeseburger called?
18. Who was the cook at the Rock and Roll Heaven diner?
19. Who invited Mary to the evening concert?
20. What was the name of the Rock and Roll Heaven maternity shop?
21. Who did Mary and Clark see hanging out outside the Rock 'Em and Sock 'Em Billiards Emporium?
22. Who was the local law in Rock and Roll Heaven?
23. Who was the mayor of Rock and Roll Heaven?
24. What was written on the side of the bus Clark crashed into while trying to flee Rock and Roll Heaven?
25. What will never die?

IV

THE NEW FILMS

TALES FROM THE DARKSIDE: THE MOVIE

Released May 1990 by Paramount
Videotape released by Paramount Home Video
Running Time: 93 minutes ("Cat From Hell,"
23 minutes).

"Qui nunc it per iter tenebricosum
Illuc, unde negeant redire quemquam."
—Catullus

The following quizzes are from the 1990 film *Tales from the Darkside: The Movie*, a feature film based on the Laurel Productions television show of the same name.

There is a ten-question quiz from the "wraparound story," which starred Blondie's Deborah Harry as a particularly nasty housewife, a ten-question quiz from the Stephen King (George Romero-scripted) segment of the film, "Cat From Hell," and a ten-question character/actor matching quiz also from the King segment.

"The Tales from the Darkside: The Movie Wraparound Story"

Quiz 12

1. Who wrote "The Wraparound Story"?
2. What was the name of Betty the cannibal's mailman?
3. What was the name of Betty the cannibal's husband?
4. What was the name of the book Betty gave the kid to read?
5. How long did it take to cook a little boy?
6. How long does evisceration take?
7. What was the first story Timmy read to Betty the cannibal?
8. What was the second story Timmy read to Betty?
9. What was the third story Timmy read to Betty?
10. How did Timmy escape from Betty the cannibal?

"Cat From Hell"
A "Cat From Hell"
Character/Actor Matching
Quiz

Quiz 13

Match the character from the left column with the actor or actress who played the role from the right column.

1. Cabbie
2. Drogan
3. Betty
4. Timmy
5. Carolyn
6. The Priest
7. Gage
8. Amanda
9. Halston
10. The Cat From Hell

A. David Forrester
B. David Johansen
C. Mark Margolis
D. Alice Drummond
E. Matthew Lawrence
F. Himself
G. Deborah Harry
H. Delores Sutton
I. William Hickey
J. Paul Greeno

"Cat From Hell"

Quiz 14

Answer the following questions from the "Cat From Hell" segment of *Tales from the Darkside: The Movie*.

1. Who paid for Halston's cab ride?
2. What was Halston's payment for the hit?
3. What did Halston call Tri-dormal-G?
4. What time did Carolyn and Amanda die?
5. Where was the veterinarian located?
6. PAUSE-BUTTON QUESTION: What kind of cereal was on the kitchen counter as Halston rummaged through the refrigerator?
7. What did Halston feel happened when you got hot?
8. How much did Halston's shirt cost?
9. What did the cat do to Halston as the hit man played pool?
10. How did the cat kill Halston?

STEPHEN KING'S "GRAVEYARD SHIFT"

Released October 26, 1990, by Paramount
Videotape released by Paramount Home Video
Running Time: 86 minutes.

"The grave's a fine and private place,
But none I think do there embrace."
—Andrew Marvell, from "To His Coy Mistress"

I gave *Stephen King's "Graveyard Shift"* a fairly
negative review in my Stephen King encyclopedia, *The
Shape Under the Sheet*, but I will admit that the second
time I saw it, I liked it better. The things I liked about
it the first time I saw it (some of the performances,
the sets), I liked even more . . . but the things I didn't
like about it (the pace, the change in the story), I *still*
didn't like.

Overall, as King fans, though, it's definitely worth
seeing, and I would suggest renting it and paying very
close attention to it so you can answer every single
one of the following questions!

(And try and get it on one of those "two night"
deals. This way you can watch the rats eat a mill
worker during *two* dinner hours instead of just one!)

(Us horror fans, huh?)

"Crypt Crawlers"

Quiz 15

A GRAVEYARD SHIFT Character/ Actor Matching Quiz

Match the character from *Stephen King's "Graveyard Shift"* from the left column with the actor or actress who played the role in the film from the right column.

_____ 1. Carmichael
_____ 2. Danson
_____ 3. John Hall
_____ 4. The Mill Inspector
_____ 5. Stevenson
_____ 6. Daisy May
_____ 7. Brogan
_____ 8. Jane Wisconsky
_____ 9. Warwick
_____10. Nardello
_____11. The Exterminator
_____12. Jason Reed
_____13. The Exterminator's Assistant
_____14. Ippeston
_____15. Warwick's Secretary

A. David Andrews
B. Emmet Kane
C. Kelly Wolf
D. Joe Perham
E. Robert Alan Beuth
F. Stephen Macht
G. Susan Lowden
H. Jimmy Woodard
I. Ilona Margolis
J. Vic Polizos
K. Kelly Goodman
L. Brad Dourif
M. Andrew Divoff
N. Minor Rootes
O. Jonathan Emerson

STEPHEN KING'S "GRAVEYARD SHIFT"

Quiz 16

1. What was the name of the waitress at the Gates Falls diner?
2. What was the name of the mill that kept Gates Falls alive and who was it named for? (WARNING: TRICK QUESTION!)
3. What was the name of the mill worker killed before the opening credits?
4. What was the name of the plant foreman?
5. How much of a bribe did the safety inspector accept from the plant foreman?
6. How did Hall get to Gates Falls?
7. What was the name of the mill where Hall had previously worked?
8. What machine did Hall start on at the mill?
9. What was Hall's starting pay at the mill?
10. What was Hall's work shift at the mill?
11. What was at least one "product placement" deal made by the producers of *Stephen King's Graveyard Shift*?
12. What was the real name of The Exterminator?
13. What company did The Exterminator work for?
14. What kind of roles did The Exterminator say Bruce Dern played?
15. What did the VC rats eat during the Vietnam War?
16. When were the sales commitments to the mill's New York office due?
17. Who strung the lights for the cleanup?

18. What was Brogan's nickname?
19. What town did Hall come from?
20. Where was Jane born?
21. Who took Stevenson's place?
22. What did Nardello do after Warwick put her on the weekend cleanup crew?
23. How much did the Fourth of July cleanup job pay?
24. Where did Hall work as a short-order cook?
25. What did Nardello steal from Warwick's desk?
26. Who manned the hose on the cleanup crew?
27. What was the name of Cleveland's dog?
28. What kind of lighter did Hall use?
29. How did Brogan die?
30. Who died after Brogan?
31. How did Warwick try to kill the rat-monster?
32. How did Jane die?
33. How did Warwick die?
34. How did the monster die?
35. How did Hall start the picker?

MISERY
Released November 1990, by Columbia Pictures
and Castle Rock Entertainment
Running Time: 105 minutes

"Nessum maggior dolore
Che ricordarsi del tempo felice
Nella miseria."
"There is no greater sorrow than to recall a time
of happiness in misery."
—Dante, *The Divine Comedy*

It doesn't get much better than this.

The film adaptation of one of Stephen King's best-loved novels proved once and for all, that first, *Stand By Me* was not a fluke, and second, that King's stories *can* be successfully brought to the screen.

This *Misery* section consists of two quizzes: "They Miserables," a character/actor matching quiz, and a forty-question quiz on the film.

"They Miserables": A MISERY Character/Actor Matching Quiz

Match the character from *Misery* from the left column with the actor or actress who played the role in the film from the right column.

_____ 1. Annie Wilkes   A. Richard Farnsworth
_____ 2. Marcia Sindell   B. Graham Jarvis
_____ 3. The Anchorman   C. Wendy Bowers
_____ 4. Buster   D. Jerry Potter
_____ 5. Libby   E. June Christopher
_____ 6. Virginia   F. Lauren Bacall
_____ 7. Paul Sheldon   G. Frances Sternhagen
_____ 8. Pete   H. Tom Brunelle
_____ 9. The   I. James Caan
       Anchorwoman   J. Kathy Bates
_____10. The Waitress

MISERY

1. What were the last words of Paul Sheldon's new, untitled novel?
2. What song was playing on his car radio as Paul drove away from the Silver Creek Lodge after he finished his new novel?
3. PAUSE-BUTTON QUESTION: What were the last three digits of the license plate number of Paul Sheldon's car?
4. What was the first printing of *Misery's Child*?
5. Who rescued Paul Sheldon after his car crash?
6. What was the name of the Silver Creek sheriff?
7. How many "Misery" novels had Annie Wilkes read?
8. What kind of champagne did Paul order before he left the Silver Creek Lodge?
9. What kind of car did Paul Sheldon drive?
10. What bothered Annie about the first forty pages of Paul's new, unpublished novel?
11. Who was Buster's deputy?
12. Who was Paul Sheldon's literary agent?
13. "What's the ceiling that dago painted?"
14. In *Misery's Child*, what year did Misery die?
15. How old was Paul when he wrote his first book?
16. Who did the audience choose?
17. What kind of typewriter did Annie buy Paul?
18. What letter was the typewriter missing?
19. What type of paper did Annie initially buy Paul?
20. What word did Paul type to show Annie that the paper smudged?

21. What did Paul use to unlock the bedroom door?
22. What was the name of Annie's scrapbook?
23. PAUSE-BUTTON QUESTION: What were the two books immediately to the right of Paul's picture (facing the picture) in Annie's living room?
24. PAUSE-BUTTON QUESTION; What was the serial number on the box of drugs Paul found in Annie's pantry as he searched the house in a wheelchair?
25. What TV show did Annie watch as Paul emptied his Novril capsules into the paper container?
26. What was the first thing (other than the smudge example) that Paul typed on the Royal?
27. Who was Annie's all-time favorite musical artist?
28. What was the name of Jim Taylor's wife?
29. What was the secret to Annie's meatloaf?
30. What did Paul take from Annie's kitchen when Annie left the house during a rainstorm?
31. How did Annie know Paul had been out of his room?
32. What did Annie use to hobble Paul?
33. In what order did Annie hobble Paul?
34. What was the quotation that allowed Buster to make the connection between Annie and Paul Sheldon?
35. Where did Annie hide Paul when Buster visited?
36. How did Paul get Buster's attention?
37. How did Buster die?
38. How did Paul *finally* kill Annie?
39. What was the title of Paul's first non-"Misery" novel?
40. After Annie was dead, where did Paul see her?

STEPHEN KING'S "IT"
An ABC Novel For Television Miniseries
Sunday, November 18, 1990
(2 hours)
Tuesday, November 20, 1990
(2 hours)

"Childhood is the kingdom where nobody dies.
Nobody that matters, that is."
  —from "Childhood Is the Kingdom Where Nobody
  Dies" by Edna St. Vincent Millay

Stephen King's "It" was a masterful adaptation of
what many consider to be one of King's most accomplished novels.

Sure, a lot was left out of the film version, but the
writers and creative team wisely did what had to be
done to make it work: They recognized and acknow-
leged that TV requires a long story to be jammed
through a funnel, so to speak, and thus, they carefully
cut the story to its bare bones.

And wonder of wonders, it worked!

I am very fond of the TV version of my favorite
Stephen King novel. I originally didn't think it could
be done in four hours. There ain't a shoehorn that
big, you know?

But I was wrong, and I'm happy I was. *Stephen
King's "It"* was absolutely terrific.

This section consists of a twenty-five-question char-
acter/actor matching quiz, and then ten questions each
for the two parts of the miniseries.

A Saunter Through the Sewers: An "It" Character/Actor Matching Quiz

Match the character from *Stephen King's "It"* from the left column with the actor or actress who played the role in the film from the right column.

_____ 1. Mrs. Kersh   A. Tim Reid
_____ 2. Ben Hanscom   B. Olivia Hussey
_____ 3. Belch Huggins   C. Tom Heaton
_____ 4. Al Marsh   D. Steven Hilton
_____ 5. Richie Tozier   E. Frank C. Turner
_____ 6. Mrs. Kaspbrak   F. Florence Patterson
_____ 7. Bill Denbrough   G. Ryan Michael
_____ 8. Mike Hanlon   H. Tony Dakota
_____ 9. Mr. Keene   I. Bill Croft
_____ 10. Sharon Denbrough   J. Caitlin Hicks
                     K. Dennis Christoper
_____ 11. Patrick Hockstetter   L. John Ritter
                     M. Gabe Khouth
_____ 12. Eddie Kaspbrak   N. Sheelah Megill
_____ 13. Chief Rademacher   O. Terence Kelly
                     P. Harry Anderson
_____ 14. Officer Nell   Q. Richard Thomas
_____ 15. Pennywise   R. Annette O'Toole
_____ 16. Tom Rogan   S. Helena Yee
_____ 17. Audra   T. Stephen Makaj
_____ 18. Ben's Father   U. Sheila Moore

_____19. Rose
_____20. Mr. Denbrough
_____21. Stan Uris
_____22. Koontz
_____23. Patty Uris
_____24. Georgie
　　　　Denbrough
_____25. Beverly Marsh

V. Scott Swanson
W. Drum Garrett
X. Richard Masur
Y. Tim Curry

STEPHEN KING'S "IT"
Part 1

Quiz 20

1. What was the name of the Derry theater?
2. Before he killed Laurie Ann, where did Pennywise hide?
3. In the novel, Stan got the first of the "Six Phone Calls." Who was first in the film?
4. TRUE OR FALSE: Bill Denbrough had a crewcut in the film.
5. What was the name of Beverly's clothing company?
6. What was the name of Eddie's wife? (WARNING: TRICK QUESTION!)
7. What was Richie Tozier's profession?
8. "Who's gonna do Carson?"
9. What TV show were Stan and his wife watching when Stan got his call?
10. What did the Losers use as bullets when they shot It?

STEPHEN KING'S "IT"
Part 2

Quiz 21

11. Who wrote *The Glowing*?
12. Who bought Silver?
13. What did the theater marquee read when Richie drove back into town?
14. Which playing cards landed face up when Bill dropped the deck Mike handed him for Silver's spokes?
15. What was the name of the director who was shooting Bill's film?
16. What was the name of the restaurant where the Losers had their reunion dinner?
17. What year was the Fire at the Black Spot?
18. "What the hell you gonna do now?"
19. TRUE OR FALSE: Eddie Kaspbrak was a virgin.
20. What happened to Eddie's body?

STEPHEN KING'S "SOMETIMES THEY COME BACK"

Originally aired on CBS, Tuesday, May 7, 1991
(2 hours)

Glendower: I can call spirits from the vasty deep.
Hotspur: Why, so can I, or so can any man;
But will they come when you do call for them?
     —William Shakespeare, from *Henry IV, Part 1*

"Stephen King's Sometimes They Come Back" was an adaptation of the *Night Shift* short story of the same name. The teleplay was by Mark Rosenthal and Lawrence Konner (*Superman IV*), and it was directed by Tom McLoughlin (*Friday the 13th, Part IV: Jason Lives* and *Date With an Angel*).

Overall, the movie was good. I found it well made, well acted, and interesting and scary. I wasn't pleased with the changes from the original story (then again, I never am), but it still held my interest for its two hours. The makeup and special effects were terrific, and generally, there was more I liked about the film than disliked, so I would definitely recommend it to King fans. (You did tape it, didn't you? If not, find someone who has it. It's worth seeing at least once.)

The happy ending was touching, and I *did* like the shift from the dark occult tone of the story to the lighter, more metaphysical *Ghost*-like feel of the movie.

This quiz section consists of a ten-question character/actor matching quiz, and then thirty questions drawn from the film version of "Sometimes They Come Back." (For questions on the original text version of the story, see the first *Stephen King Quiz Book*.)

70

"On The Night Shift":
A "SOMETIMES THEY COME BACK" Character/Actor Matching Quiz

Quiz 22

Match the character from "Stephen King's Sometimes They Come Back" from the left column with the actor or actress who played the role in the film from the right column.

____ 1. Sally Norman	A William Sanderson
____ 2. Kate	B. Brooke Adams
____ 3. Carl Mueller	C. T. Max Graham
____ 4. Richard Lawson	D. William Kuhlke
____ 5. Officer Nell	E. Tasia Valenza
____ 6. Jim Norman	F. Nancy McLoughlin
____ 7. Chief Pappas	G. Duncan McLeod
____ 8. Dr. Bernardi	H. Chad Nyerges
____ 9. Principal Simmons	I. Nicholas Sadler
____10. Chip	J. Tim Matheson

Stephen King's "Sometimes They Come Back"

Quiz 23

1. What was the name of Jim's wife?
2. What was the name of their son?
3. Who warned Jim to pass the jocks on Jim's first day of class?
4. Who apologized to Jim for the jocks' behavior?
5. What was the name of the high school football team?
6. How long had Jim's childhood home been deserted?
7. When Jim took a fantasy trip back to his old house, what TV show was playing in the living room?
8. How much is $3 \times 2 \times 2$?
9. PAUSE-BUTTON QUESTION: What book did Jim drop when he was grabbed by the hoods in the tunnel?
10. What did Billy Sterns drop in the school parking lot as he rode away from Jim's van?
11. How did Billy Sterns die?
12. Who was Jim's first back-from-the-dead transfer student?
13. What did Chip throw at Jim in class?
14. What other Stephen King film did Brooke Adams appear in?
15. What did the hoods do to Kate?
16. Where did Chip's brother live?
17. What was the name of the police chief who questioned Jim?

18. What did the back-from-the-dead hoods do to Chip to make sure he was *really* scared?
19. Who was Jim's third back-from-the-dead transfer student?
20. What did Jim give to Scott after the hoods tried to run the boy down?
21. What was the name of the retired officer Jim went to see about the hoods?
22. What other Stephen King work does this officer appear in?
23. Where did the punks transfer from?
24. What was the name of the hood who didn't die in the train wreck?
25. What happened when Jim shot Lawson six times?
26. What did the punks do to Jim's van?
27. What happened to Lawson when he stepped into the church?
28. How did Mueller die?
29. What happened to Wayne after the hell-train killed the hoods?
30. What did Jim give Scotty after Wayne "left"?

STEPHEN KING'S
"GOLDEN YEARS"

"The world's great age begins anew,
The golden years return . . ."
                —from "Hellas" by Percy Bysshe Shelley

"Stephen King's Golden Years" is the story of a mild-mannered janitor named Harlan Williams who one day is caught in an explosion at the agricultural testing facility where he works. From that moment on, he begins to grow younger . . . and the government wants to keep him under lock and key. There is a particularly lovely government agent in the series who decides to help Harl and his wife, and a particularly mean and nasty one (a *Shop* agent nonetheless!) who wants to erase *all* evidence of the accident. The series also introduced us to a gen-yoo-wyne mad scientist, a blind female activist, a character from an early King work (and another one with the nickname of a character from an important King novel), and a cameo by King himself.

The pace of the series was leisurely. (One well-known writer who has done books about King told me he thought it was "glacial.") But I found myself getting completely caught up in the story, and (in what I suppose is the ultimate test of a good tale) wanting it to continue past its conclusion. I wanted to know more about these people and what happened to them in the story, and that seems to me to be a good sign that we have, indeed, experienced a story well-told.

But then what else can we expect from Stephen King? Right? Right.

Now before I turn you over to these questions, I must also say that the choice of theme song for the series was absolutely perfect! (And I would have mentioned the name of the song, but then I would have been giving away the first question!)

This quiz consists of a thirty-question character/actor matching quiz, and then 123 questions drawn from the seven episodes of Stephen King's 1991 CBS summer series "Golden Years."

There are questions from each episode, and the queries are in (mostly) chronological order.

It might help to watch your videotapes of the episodes before taking the quiz. (You *did* tape them for your King collection, didn't you?) Some of the questions require a very close watching of the series.

STEPHEN KING'S "GOLDEN YEARS"
WHO RUNS FOR THE SHADOWS IN THESE GOLDEN YEARS?
A Character/Actor Matching Quiz

Quiz 24

Match the character from "Stephen King's Golden Years" from the left column with the actor or actress who played the role in the series from the right column.

_____ 1. The Pilot
_____ 2. Steven Dent
_____ 3. Redding
_____ 4. Gina Williams
_____ 5. The Bus Driver
_____ 6. Dr. Eakins
_____ 7. Harlan Williams
_____ 8. Dr. Ackerman's Nurse
_____ 9. Yaniger
_____10. The Janitor
_____11. The Trucker
_____12. Major Moreland
_____13. General Louis Crewes
_____14. Cap'n Trips
_____15. Ernie

A. Keith Szarabajka
B. Frances Sternhagen
C. Felicity Huffman
D. Bill Raymond
E. R. D. Call
F. Ed Lauter
G. Matt Molloy
H. Adam Redfield
I. John Rothman
J. Stephen Root
K. J. R. Horne
L. Graham Paul
M. Peter McRobbie
N. Phil Lenkowsky
O. Brad Greenquist
P. Mert Hatfield
Q. Michael P. Moran

EPISODE 1
(2 hours)
Originally broadcast Tuesday, July 16, 1991

Quiz 25

"**Debut:** Stephen King created (and wrote the first five episodes of) this seven-part series about the fall-out from a botched experiment that contaminates and oddly affects an elderly janitor at an Agricultural Department 'testing facility' "—*TV Guide*, July 13–19, 1991.

1-1. What was the theme song to "Stephen King's Golden Years"?

1-2. What was the name of the gatekeeper at the agricultural testing facility where Harlan worked?

1-3. How old was Harlan at the beginning of the series?

1-4. When was Harlan's birthday, and how old would he be?

1-5. What two forms of identification did the agricultural testing facility's gate computer require for entrance?

1-6. What was the name of the agricultural testing facility?

1-7. What color was Harlan's bike?

1-8. What was the price tag of the agricultural testing facility's particle accelerator?

1-9. What was Harlan's ID number?

1-10. Before the turbine explosion, which switch was showing a red light on Todhunter's control board?

1-11. Which of Todhunter's assistants initially convinced the doctor to abort the gold series test?

1-12. What was Harlan's co-worker Billy's new hobby?

1-13. What kind of computers did the secretaries in Major Moreland's office use?

1-14. Before the explosion, why did Major Moreland call Harlan into his office?

1-15. Who was Head of Security at the agricultural testing facility?

1-16. Who was in charge of the agricultural testing facility?

1-17. What was the name of Harlan's wife?

1-18. What was ostensibly the focus of Dr. Todhunter's experiments?

1-19. What was the green stuff?

1-20. What happened to the scar on Redding's calf just before he died?

1-21. What was the name of the Shop agent assigned to the investigation at the agricultural testing facility?

1-22. What doctor gave Harlan a clean bill of health after the explosion?

1-23. What was Harlan's middle name?

1-24. What did Dr. Eakins notice about Harlan's eyes during his second eye exam?

1-25. What happened to Lieutenant McGiver before he testified about the explosion?

1-26. When was new software issued to secretaries at the agricultural testing facility?

1-27. Where did Andrews keep his phone line scrambler?

1-28. What kind of lighter did Andrews use?

1-29. After the improvement in his eyesight, what was the *next* improvement in Harlan's physical condition?

1-30. Where did Harlan's co-worker Billy go to high school? (WARNING: TRICK QUESTION!)

EPISODE 2
(1 hour)
Originally broadcast Thursday, July 18, 1991

Quiz 26

"Harlan and Gina face strange changes in him, and the possibility that he may be in danger, while Jude rolls on with his sinister 'special assignment' to keep the facts about the accident from surfacing."—*TV Guide*, July 13–19, 1991.

2-1. What kind of lighter did Dr. Mark Ackerman use?

2-2. How much did Harlan's visual acuity improve on his second eye test?

2-3. Who did Dr. Todhunter's watch originally belong to?

2-4. What did Jude Andrews make for breakfast in Dr. Ackerman's house?

2-5. What sign did Jude Andrews once see on a desk that he thought made perfect sense?

2-6. What did Andrews threaten to do to Dr. Ackerman if he found out that the doctor withheld information from him?

2-7. What did Harlan tell Rick was his secret to feeling and looking so good?

2-8. "Why did the man tie his watch to a bird?"

2-9. What were "fruits and nuts"?

2-10. What was the name of the salon where Harlan

went to have his hair colored back to all white?

2-11. What was the name of the hairstylist who took care of Harlan's "reverse" hair dye job?

2-12. Who killed Dr. Eakins?

2-13. Where did Harlan tell his wife to put the two packed suitcases?

2-14. Where were the three places the Shop had where people could "disappear"?

2-15. What sudden, sad realization came to Harlan's wife as she and Harlan were dancing in the living room?

EPISODE 3
(1 hour)
Originally broadcast Thursday, July 25, 1991

Quiz 27

"Sensing the growing danger to Harlan, Terry convinces him and Gina to leave with her—right away; but Andrews is after them."—*TV Guide*, July 20–26, 1991.

3-1. In her apartment, where did Terry hide her gun?

3-2. What code did Terry use to give Crewes the phone number where he could call her on the night she found out about Dr. Eakins's murder?

3-3. What was Terry's coded message to Crewes?

3-4. What was the name of the photographer who took the pictures of Eakins's murder scene?

3-5. What newspaper did the crime scene photographer work for?

3-6. What time was Dr. Eakins's body found?

3-7. Before Eakins's murder, how long had it been since there was a premeditated murder in Falco Plains?

3-8. Who did the scene postmortem on Dr. Eakins?

3-9. What did the cops do with Dr. Eakins's body?

3-10. Who killed Steven Dent?

3-11. Where was the listening bug planted in Harlan's house?

3-12. What message did Terry leave for Jude in Harlan's house?

3-13. Where did Francie live?

3-14. What was the name of Francie's seeing-eye dog?

3-15. Where did Terry steal the hearse?

EPISODE 4
(1 hour)
Originally broadcast Thursday, August 1, 1991

Quiz 28

"On the run, on the road, Harlan's reverse aging begins to alienate Gina; another person-in-the-know is knocked off, and Jude takes official control of the investigation; and Dr. Todhunter becomes a slightly looser cannon."—*TV Guide*, July 27–August 2, 1991.

4-1. What color did Terry and Harlan paint the hearse?

4-2. Who did the corpse look like?

4-3. What was the name of the mummy Harlan and his wife saw at Coney Island?

4-4. How did Dr. Ackerman die?

4-5. What did Crewes do with the bottle of whiskey from which Andrews took a slug?

4-6. Who did people in the Shop think was the best field operative that had ever lived?

4-7. Who did Terry think was better than this "best ever" field operative?

4-8. Where did Todhunter sleep the night he told his "only living record" mouse that he was taking it to his house?

4-9. Why wouldn't Rick let General Crewes through the front gate of the agricultural testing facility?

4-10. What was the key element in Terry's plan to protect Harlan and his wife from the Shop?

4-11. What was the downside of Terry's plan?

4-12. How did Todhunter's "fountain of youth" mice die?

4-13. What was Billy planning to do with Todhunter's dead mice?

4-14. How did Terry sneak up on the State Trooper?

4-15. Where did the State Trooper keep his spare handcuff key?

EPISODE 5
(1 hour)
Originally broadcast Thursday, August 8, 1991

Quiz 29

"Harlan separates from Terry and Gina to keep Andrews off course, and they plan to meet again in Chicago; Gen. Crewes asserts himself and races to get vital data on Harlan before Andrews. Stephen King has a cameo."—*TV Guide*, August 3–9, 1991.

5-1. What was the code word Andrews had to say before Captain Marsh would fill him in on the situation with the cruiser?

5-2. What did Andrews tell Marsh to do with Gina and Terry?

5-3. What was the "shooting configuration" Marsh assigned to his men?

5-4. What did Terry and company plant in the ditched cruiser?

5-5. Who played the bus driver on Gina and Terry's Chicago-bound bus?

5-6. What did Terry tell the bus driver to do?

5-7. What was the name of Major Moreland's secretary?

5-8. Who gave Harlan a ride?

5-9. What database in Central Records held Harlan's file?

5-10. Who did Andrews order to find Harlan's file in Central Records?

5-11. What was the code word Moreland used to "lockout" Harlan's file?

5-12. Why didn't Moreland want to go to Chicago?

5-13. How did General Crewes get out of the agricultural testing facility?

5-14. What happened when Harlan fell asleep in the truck on the way to Chicago?

5-15. What did the trucker say as he leaped from the truck in terror just before the earthquake?

EPISODE 6
(1 hour)
Originally broadcast Thursday, August 15, 1991

Quiz 30

"The crisis takes its toll on Gina as she and Terry make it to Francie's in Chicago, while Harlan, Andrews, and Gen. Crewes also head for the Windy City."—*TV Guide*, August 10–16, 1991.

6-1. Who did Todhunter call "The Grand Watchmaker"?

6-2. According to Jude Andrews, what did he think there should be laws against?

6-3. What was Billy's sixth lesson?

6-4. Where did Douglas Williams live?

6-5. Where did Thomas Williams live?

6-6. What was the number of the bus that took Gina and Terry to Chicago?

6-7. What was Francie's apartment number?

6-8. At what level of his experiment did Dr. Todhunter fire his team?

6-9. What did Harlan order in the diner on his way to Chicago?

6-10. What happened to Harlan in the diner?

6-11. Who did Terry call a "blind female Don Rickles"?

6-12. What was Francie "allergic" to?

6-13. What did Jude Andrews do to the Chicago

cop who delayed him on his way to Francie's apartment?

6-14. What happened to Whitney?

6-15. What was the license number of Harlan and company's "escape car"?

EPISODE 7
(1 hour)
Originally broadcast Thursday, August 22, 1991

Quiz 31

"The climax in Chicago: Andrews prepares for a final assault; Gen. Crewes links up with Terry and they accept Francie's offer to hide them along with Harlan and ailing Gina at a safe house. Meanwhile, Dr. Todhunter gets amazing results as he continues his experiments. [Last scheduled show.]"—*TV Guide*, August 17–23, 1991.

7-1. What was the name of the woman who cooked for Terry and company at the safe house?

7-2. What was the name of the fake ID guy who lived in Wisconsin?

7-3. What was Cap'n Trips Shop operative number?

7-4. What happened to Dr. Todhunter's clock?

7-5. What color was Gina's dress that night in Baltimore?

7-6. How much did Gina's "Baltimore" outfit cost?

7-7. Why was Terry still alive?

7-8. What did the Shop agents unload from the garbage truck?

7-9. What did Andrews threaten to do to Burton if he didn't deliver the city plans?

7-10. What did Gina believe?

7-11. How did Major Moreland die?

7-12. How did Tom and Sybil die?

7-13. How did Cap'n Trips die?
7-14. How was Harlan captured?
7-15. What was Gina's last word?

(A Drawing of) Three Bonus Questions

7-16. According to Todhunter, what singular distinction did Harlan hold?
7-17. While under sedation at Falco Plains, what did Harlan mumble?
7-18. What David Bowie quote ended the seven-episode run of the series?

Golden Reflections: An Afterthought

When "Stephen King's Golden Years" was first announced, the hype was that the network—and King—weren't sure if the series would continue past its seven-episode summer run. If the ratings were good, we were told, then there was an opportunity for the story to continue as a regular series.

Knowing that, my reaction after the sixth (the next-to-last) episode, was that King had a whole boatload of loose ends to tie up in the final episode. My thinking was that "Golden Years" was originally intended to stand as an independent miniseries, and that we could therefore expect a beginning, a middle, and most important, an end to the series: a satisfying conclusion that answered all of the questions raised during the summer run of "Golden Years."

Instead of a denouement that satisfied, however, we got a cliff-hanger that antagonized. Did everyone involved really plan on the series being a regular part of CBS's fall schedule, and thus, there was no need for a resolution? Who knows? What we do know is that several questions were left unanswered.

Questions like:

• How young will Harlan get?
• Why did Harlan cause earthquakes?

- What happened to Gina?
- Why did the sun come up at midnight, and was it due to Harlan?
- How did time travel figure into Todhunter's experiments?
- How did Terry get so tough?
- Will Jude Andrews get his one day?

Instead of answers to these questions, however, we got a cliff-hanger and a "To be continued . . ." on the screen. Episode 7 ended with Harlan in captivity (under Andrews's [and it is assumed, Todhunter's] control and tied to a bed no less), Gina dead, Major Moreland dead, Burton still possessing his ear (and his other twistable body parts), Cap'n Trips dead, and Terry and Crewes on the run.

How much more of the story is written has not been announced, but we can only hope that when (and if) the story becomes a regular series, we'll have our questions answered.

Until then, stay tuned!

(I guess.)

V

MISCELLANEOUS FILM QUIZZES

"WHO PLAYED WHO?"

Quiz 32

Match the actors in Column 1 with the Stephen King characters they played from Column 2, and the films in which they appeared from Column 3.

_____ 1. David Johansen   A. Beverly Marsh   a. *The Dead Zone*

_____ 2. Alan King   B. Hendershot

      C. Leigh Cabot   b. *Carrie*

_____ 3. Shelley Duvall   D. Chris Hargensen   c. *'Salem's Lot*

_____ 4. Alexandra Paul   E. Larry Crockett   d. *Sorry, Right Number*

      F. Burt Stanton

_____ 5. Nancy Allen   G. Gordie Lachance   e. *Maximum Overdrive*

_____ 6. Deborah Harmon   H. Mrs. Cavanaugh   f. *Firestarter*

_____ 7. Annette O'Toole   I. Wendy Torrance   g. *Children of the Corn*

_____ 8. Drew Barrymore   J. Stevie   h. *Christine*

      K. Tad Trenton   i. *Cat From Hell*

_____ 9. Danny Pintauro   L. Halston   j. *Creepshow 2*

_____10. Richard Dreyfuss   M. John Elliott

      N. Marcia Sindell   k. *Stand By Me*

_____11. Fred Willard   O. Charlie McGee   l. *Silver Bullet*

_____12. Lauren Bacall   P. The Minister

      Q. Dr. Donatti   m. *Cat's Eye*

_____13. Colleen Dewhurst   R. Henrietta Dodd   n. *Cujo*

95

_____14. Stephen   S. Marty Coslaw   o. *The*
       King   T. Katie   *Shining*
_____15. Peter   Weiderman   p. *The*
       Horton   *Woman*
_____16. Michael   *in the*
       Cornelison   *Room*
_____17. Pat Hingle   q. *The Run-*
_____18. Corey   *ning Man*
       Haim   r. *Pet*
_____19. Dweezil   *Sematary*
       Zappa   s. *It*
_____20. Shirley   t. *Misery*
       Sonderegger

"DIRECTED BY . . ."

Quiz 33

Match the director from Column 1 with the film he or she directed in Column 2.

_____ 1. Tommy Lee Wallace

_____ 2. Tobe Hooper

_____ 3. Daniel Attias

_____ 4. John Carpenter

_____ 5. Lewis Teague

_____ 6. David Cronenberg

_____ 7. Frank Darabont

_____ 8. Michael Gornick

_____ 9. Brian De Palma

_____10. Mary Lambert

_____11. George Romero

_____12. Stanley Kubrick

_____13. Fritz Kiersch

_____14. Jim Cole

_____15. Rob Reiner

_____16. Stephen King

_____17. Ralph S. Singleton

_____18. John Harrison

_____19. Brett Leonard

_____20. Paul Michael Glaser

A. *The Dead Zone*
B. *Christine*
C. *Stephen King's "It"*
D. *Cujo*
E. *Tales from the Darkside: The Movie*
F. *The Shining*
G. *Pet Sematary*
H. *The Lawnmower Man*
I. *Maximum Overdrive*
J. *'Salem's Lot*
K. *Carrie*
L. *Creepshow*
M. *Stand By Me*
N. *Creepshow 2*
O. *Misery*
P. *Children of the Corn*
Q. *The Last Rung on the Ladder*
R. *The Running Man*
S. *The Woman in the Room*
T. *Stephen King's "Graveyard Shift"*
U. *Cat's Eye*
V. *Silver Bullet*

"I LIKE TO WATCH . . ."

Quiz 34

As all good popular culture "residents" should, Stephen King's characters watch TV, read magazines, and, yup, go to the movies and watch videos. This quiz asks you to match the movie seen from "The Movies" column with the character watching it from "The Watchers" column and the Stephen King work in which they appear from "The Works" column.

The Movies

_____ 1. *In the Heat of the Night*
_____ 2. *The Bank Dick*
_____ 3. *I Was a Teenage Frankenstein*
_____ 4. *. . . And Justice for All*
_____ 5. *Hell's Angels on Wheels*
_____ 6. *Citizen Kane*
_____ 7. *White Line Fever*
_____ 8. *Child's Play*
_____ 9. *Bambi*
_____10. *Grease*

The Watchers

A. Sarah Bracknell and John Smith
B. Paul Sheldon
C. Vic, Donna, and Tad Trenton
D. Meg Delevan
E. Frannie Goldsmith
F. Heidi and Billy Halleck
G. Richard Wentworth

H. Dennis Guilder and Roseanne
I. Richie, Ben, and Beverly
J. Eddie Dean

The Works

a. *It*
b. *Thinner*
c. *Christine*
d. "Something to Tide You Over"
e. *The Stand*
f. *The Dead Zone*
g. *Misery*
h. "The Sun Dog"
i. *Cujo*
j. *The Dark Tower II: The Drawing of the Three*

VI

A
QUANTITY
OF
QUINTESSENTIAL
QUERIES
AND
QUIZZES

Lies, Guts, Quotes, Notes, Titles, & Vitals

"WHO SAID IT?"

Quiz 35

"Bright is the ring of words
  When the right man rings them . . ."
    —Robert Louis Stevenson, from *Songs of Travel*

"Footfalls echo in the memory
Down the passage which we did not take
Towards the door we never opened
Into the rose-garden. My words echo
Thus, in your mind.
              —T. S. Eliot, from *Four Quartets*,
                "Burnt Norton"

"What do you say?"
    —John Lennon and Paul McCartney, from "Hey
        Bulldog," the *Yellow Submarine* album

Match the dialogue spoken with the person who said it. (To help you spear the speaker, the stories in which the speeches were spoken are specified. See? Si.)

_____ 1. "A little of everything, that's what a successful business is all about, Brian. Diversity, pleasure, amazement, fulfillment . . . what a successful *life* is all about, for that matter . . . I don't give advice, but if I did, you could do worse than to remember that . . ."

_____ 2. "I was running *stuff* for Will. I only moved coke for him once or twice, and I thank

Christ that I didn't have anything worse than untaxed cigarettes when they picked me up."

_____ 3. "Do you know my daddy once owned all this land for miles around? It's true. No small trick for a black man. And I played my guitar and sang down at the Grange Hall in nineteen and oh-two. Long ago, Nick. Long, long ago."

_____ 4. *"Larry! The rung! It's letting go!"*

_____ 5. "Here, sir, there are *always* more tales."

_____ 6. Well, you know, ma'am, we're real far out in the boonies here, and attractin' an audience is kinda slow work . . . although once they hear us, *ever*body stays around for more . . . and we was kinda hopin' you'd stick around yourselves for a while."

_____ 7. "The soil of a man's heart is stonier, Louis. A man grows what he can . . . and tends it."

_____ 8. "On the island we always watched out for our own. When Gerd Henreid broke the blood vessel in his chest that time, we had covered-dish suppers one whole summer to pay for his operation in Boston—and Gerd came back alive, thank God."

_____ 9. "You take your *requests*, and you jam them up your nose with the rest of the boogers, my dear little prince. And the next time you call me in here for any such royal rubbage as *this*, you'll bleed for it.

_____10. "This is just a needle, but it *is* steel and it should serve our purpose as well as a compass. The Beam is our course now, and the needle will show it."

_____11. "We're going to reach an understanding. We're going to have a little seminar right here in this back room about just who's the asshole. You got my meaning? We're gonna reach some conclusions. Isn't that what you college boys like to do? Reach conclusions?"

_____12. "When this is all over, I'm going to write a book."

_____13. "Time will tell, I suppose. For now, I'd advise you to stick to the line you took with me last night—this is a guy who *thinks* he's George Stark, and he's crazy enough to have started at the logical place—logical for a crazyman, anyway—the place where Stark was officially buried."

_____14. "*Oooog! Oooog!* Blood! *Ooooog*, blood! *Blood!*"

_____15. "I'm thinking of writing a book about the Overlook Hotel. I thought if I actually got through it, the owner of the scrapbook would like to have an acknowledgment at the front."

_____16. *"You can't hurt me! You're afraid of me! Besides, you liked it! You LIKED it! YOU DIRTY LITTLE BOY, YOU LIKED IT!"*

_____17. "Davvey Ardwell wadda main who walk lak e ohn heffa de worl an haddim a daylah on de resp."

_____18. "Oh Jacky, it's a Pit. Furnaces of the Black Heart down there. Black Heart at the middle of the world. Can't stay, Jacky, it's the worst bad there is."

_____19. "Listen to me, you chicken-fried son of a bitch. I missed getting turned into strawberry jam by that 727 because your shit genny didn't kick in when it was supposed to; as a result I had no ATC comm. I don't know how many people on the *airliner* just missed getting turned into strawberry jam, but I bet *you* do, and I know the cockpit crew does. The only reason those guys are still alive is because the captain of that boat was bright enough to allemande right, and I was bright enough to do-si-do, but I have sustained both structural and physical damage. If you don't give me a landing clearance right now, I'm going to land, anyway. The only difference is that if I have to land without clearance, I'm going to have you up in front of an FAA hearing. But first I will personally see to it that your head and your asshole change places. Have you got that, *hoss*?"

_____20. *"He stole me, Popsy! He stole me, he stole me, the bad man stole me!"*

Bonus Quotation

(No corresponding match is supplied for this quote. The speaker must be identified without any clues.)

21. "Listen, you stupid cull, and listen well, for this is your last warning. You yank that fucking street-head off right now or I'll reach into your mouth and rip the living tongue right out of it. And feel free to bite all you want while I do it, for what I have runs in the blood and you'll see the first blossoms on yer own face before the weeks out— if yer lives that long."

A. The Kid (Popsy's grandson), "Popsy"
B. Egbert Thoroughgood, *It*
C. Roland, *The Dark Tower III: The Waste Lands*
D. Greg Stillson, *The Dead Zone*
E. Mother Abagail, *The Stand: The Complete & Uncut Edition*
F. Leland Gaunt, *Needful Things*
G. Kitty, "The Last Rung on the Ladder"
H. Stella Flanders, "The Reach"
I. Victor Pascow, *Pet Sematary*
J. Harkness, *The Long Walk*
K. The Library Policeman, "The Library Policeman"
L. Alan Pangborn, *The Dark Half*
N. Richard Dees, "The Night Flier"
O. Jack Torrance, *The Shining*
P. LaVerne, "The Raft"
Q. Beson, *The Eyes of the Dragon*
R. Stevens, "The Breathing Method"
S. Elvis Presley, "You Know They Got a Hell of a Band"
T. Arnie Cunningham, *Christine*

"Crossover Dreams"

Quiz 36

Stephen King's characters (and locales, for that matter; most notably Castle Rock, Maine) often show up in several different works, often enough, in fact, for me to wonder (occasionally aloud, too) if King is just writing one huge novel and breaking it up into yearly volumes!

This quiz asks you to match the characters from the left column with the *works* (notice I used the plural) in which they appear from the right column.

Seven of the characters listed appear in two King works; two appear in three, and one guy shows up in a whopping four different King stories.

____ 1. Reginald "Pop" Merrill

____ 2. Jack Sawyer

____ 3. Bobbi Anderson

____ 4. Mrs. Kaspbrak

____ 5. Richard Dees

____ 6. Randall Flagg

____ 7. Joe Camber

____ 8. Ace Merrill

____ 9. Frank Dodd

____ 10. Sheriff Alan Pangborn

A. "The Night Flier"
B. "The Sun Dog"
C. *Cujo*
D. *The Talisman*
E. *The Dark Tower II: The Drawing of the Three*
F. *Needful Things*
G. *The Tommyknockers*
H. *The Stand: The Complete & Uncut Edition*
I. *The Stand*
J. "The Body"
K. *The Dark Half*
L. *The Dead Zone*
M. *It*
N. *The Eyes of the Dragon*
O. *Misery*

"BORN IN THE USA"
A Stephen King Map Quiz

Quiz 37

Match the following descriptions with the proper location numbers from the "Stephen King's America" map.

_____A. George Stark's birthplace, according to his Darwin Press bio sheet.

_____B. This was where the Bannings had their farm.

_____C. The location of the Free Zone.

_____D. After they were married, Stan and Patty Uris lived in a suburb of this southern town.

_____E. A city where Red Razberry Zingers were successfully test marketed.

_____F. Mother Abagail's birthplace.

_____G. The location of the Shop.

_____H. Morgan Sloat's birthplace.

_____I. The town where "the Calmative" was discovered.

_____J. The town where Thad Beaumont was born.

_____K. The town where Christine "lived."

_____L. The town where Dick Hallorann spent the winter season.

_____M. The town where Annie Wilkes and her brother Paul went to the movies every Saturday afternoon.

_____N. George Stark's final residence, according to his Darwin Press bio sheet.

_____O. Stephen King's hometown.

1. Hemingford Home, Nebraska.
2. Troy, New York.
3. Boulder, Colorado.
4. Bergenfield, New Jersey.
5. Manchester, New Hampshire.
6. Bangor, Maine.
7. St. Petersburg, Florida.
8. Bakersfield, California.
9. Oxford, Mississippi.
10. La Plata, Texas.
11. Akron, Ohio.
12. Boise, Idaho.
13. Longmont, Virginia.
14. Atlanta, Georgia.
15. Libertyville, Pennsylvania.

"MORE TRUTH ... MORE LIES"

Quiz 38

Answer true or false to the following statements about Stephen King's novels, novellas, and short stories.

1. Carrie White got her first menstrual period during a shower after gym class.
2. The Alhambra Inn and Gardens was in Nevada.
3. The Bradley Gang was executed in October of 1979 in Derry, Maine.
4. When Andy Dufresne revamped the Shawshank Prison library, he included a selection of Stephen King novels.
5. Carlos Detweiller wrote *True Tales of Demon Infestations*.
6. The Mangler lived in the Blue Ribbon Laundry.
7. Gold was $750 an ounce when Richard Hagstrom created a bag of gold coins with his word processor.
8. Stephen King wrote the short story "Never Look Behind You" with Chris Chesley.
9. George Stark's epitaph was "What Are You Looking At?"
10. "Eye of the Crow" was written by Mort Rainey. (WARNING: TRICK QUESTION!)
11. In Woody Allen's film *The Purple Rose of Cairo*, a character steps out of the screen and into a woman's life. (And this *does* have something to do with Stephen King, I swear.)
12. Uncle Al always came to Tarker's Mills in July for the traditional antipasto and manicotti dinner with Marty's family.

13. After the rook raiser began raising rooks in Bangor, Maine, the London City Council sent him a telegram every day that said, "Bred Any Good Rooks Lately?"
14. Miss Eleusippus Deere and Mrs. Meleusippus Verrill lived in Portland, Maine.
15. Garrish the sniper's roommate was Richie Tozier.
16. Danny Torrance had "the shining."
17. Anders Peyna was the manifestation of Flagg two hundred fifty years before King Roland's reign.
18. Victor Pascow's last words were "It's not the real cemetery."
19. Judge Cary Rossington once grabbed Heidi Halleck's "oh-so-grabbable-tit" during a New Year's Eve kiss.
20. Christine was a 1963 yellow Ford Thunderbird.
21. Brother Zeno was shot for treason.
22. Louis and Margaret Godlin begat Stella Godlin, who became Stella Flanders.
23. The "hero" in Reg Thorpe's short story, "The Ballad of the Flexible Bullet," dumped strawberry Jell-O on a fat girl's head, and then killed his wife and baby daughter.
24. After Jake's death, the Man in Black took Roland to Golgotha for a palaver.
25. "[F]iction is the truth inside the lie, and the truth of this fiction is simple enough: *the magic exists.*"

"STILL SHAKIN'!"

Quiz 39

Rearrange the following jumbles into the titles of some of Stephen King's novels, short stories, and non-fiction articles. All the letters in the titles have been placed in like groups, in alphabetical order, which tends to render this quiz particularly difficult. But you're up to it . . . ain't ya? (There are twenty Difficult jumbles here [well, some aren't *that* hard!], and just to spice things up a little bit, one Ridiculously Difficult jumble. So, A E F H N U V!)

1. A DDD EEE H R T X
2. AA D F H II MM N O P R SS TTT U
3. E F OO N R W
4. AAA DD EEE HH III O L RR SS TTTT WW
5. A DD EEEEE F HH I J LLL M N OOOO RRR TT V Y
6. A E G R
7. AAAA C D H I NN O P R T
8. C K R S T U
9. CC EEEE FF H LL OO R T WW Y
10. D EE F G H I L NN S T U
11. AAA BB C D EE G I MM NNNN O R
12. A E F H R TT
13. E I M R S Y
14. AA EE M P R S TT Y
15. E H I M S TT
16. C E II N Q R S TT U
17. A EE G H I LL N O R S T
18. C EE H O P R S W

112

19. A D E L S
20. C J O U

"The Ridiculously Difficult Jumble"

21. AAAA BB D EEE GGGGG H K MM NN
    OOOOOOOOO P R SS TTTT UUU Y

"WHO'S WHO?" II

Quiz 40

Match the Stephen King character from the left column with the Stephen King work in which he, she, or it appears from the right column.

_____ 1. Marcia Cressner
_____ 2. Bow-Wow Fornoy
_____ 3. Craig Toomy
_____ 4. Nathan Grantham
_____ 5. Hubie Marsten
_____ 6. Beverly Marsh
_____ 7. Cathy Scott
_____ 8. Sandy Galton
_____ 9. Kennerly
_____10. Rita Blakemoor
_____11. Irma Fayette
_____12. Kevin Delevan
_____13. Tommy Ross
_____14. George Stark
_____15. Ronnie Hanelli
_____16. Maddie Pace
_____17. Steve Kemp
_____18. Dr. Pedersen
_____19. Violet Mitla
_____20. Maureen Scollay
_____21. Clive Banning
_____22. The Major
_____23. Adelle Frawley
_____24. Dave Duncan

A. "Father's Day"
B. *Christine*
C. *Carrie*
D. *It*
E. *The Dark Half*
F. "Survivor Type"
G. "The Langoliers"
H. *The Shining*
I. "The Ledge"
J. *The Stand: The Complete & Uncut Edition*
K. "The Wedding Gig"
L. "Here There Be Tygers"
M. *The Eyes of the Dragon*
N. *'Salem's Lot*
O. "The End of the Whole Mess"
P. "The Moving Finger"
Q. *The Stand*
R. "Something to Tide You Over"
S. *Thinner*
T. "The Sun Dog"
U. "My Pretty Pony"

114

"TITLE SEARCH":
A First Letters Quiz

Quiz 41

The first letters of the correct responses to the sixteen questions in this quiz spell out something quite important to buyers of *The Stephen King Quiz Book(s)*!

1. Danny Torrance had the ? _____
2. ". . .'cause I'm so afraid of the ? man" _____
3. Flagg would look through the ? _____
4. Louis buried Creed in the ? _____
5. Halston was done in by the cat from ? _____
6. Lonnie Freeman got lost in Crouch ? _____
7. The precursor to *The Stand* was ? _____
8. Clues 8–12? _____
9. Odetta was part of the ? _____
10. Ray Garraty "won" the Long ? _____
11. Pennywise was ? _____
12. Dwight Renfield, aka the ? _____
13. Ed Hamner told Elizabeth I ? _____
14. Arthur told Richard, "?" _____
15. "Do you love?" was asked by ? _____
16. Roland was the last ? _____

"POISON AIR"
The Music of Stephen King

Quiz 42

The title of this quiz comes from something Stephen King once said in an interview. When describing the way he wrote, he said when he enters his office, he puts on rock and roll so loud it "poisons the air." He said this tended to keep people away from his side of the house, and thus, he wasn't distracted from his work.

This quiz asks you to match Stephen King's use of music in his stories with where or how the song(s) or group(s) were used. To make it easier, the title of the work in which the piece (or people) appears is also given, so all you have to do is go look it up. (Or you can always cheat.)

_____ 1. Leadbelly tunes.

_____ 2. A polka with French lyrics.

_____ 3. "Leaning on the Everlasting Arms."

_____ 4. "I Got a Telephone Call from Heaven and Jesus Was on the Line."

_____ 5. "King Creole" by Elvis Presley.

_____ 6. The National Anthem, a medley of Sousa marches, and "Marching to Pretoria."

_____ 7. "Thank God I'm a Country Boy" by John Denver.

_____ 8. "Born on the Bayou" by John Fogerty.

_____ 9. Jefferson Airplane's "Long John Silver" album.

_____ 10. "Blue Danube Waltz"

_____11. "She's Got To Be a Saint" by Ray Price.

_____12. "The First Noël."

_____13. "Sherry" by the Four Seasons.

_____14. "Maybelline" by Chuck Berry.

_____15. The Beach Boys.

_____16. "I'm Gonna Charleston Back To Charleston."

_____17. Bach and Brahms.

_____18. Muzak.

_____19. A Bo Diddley cassette.

_____20. "End of the World Suite Arranged for Clock-Work Figures."

_____21. "Beulah Land."

_____22. "Alfie."

_____23. "The Horst Wessel Song."

_____24. "Hey Jude" by The Beatles.

_____25. "Baby, Can You Dig Your Man?"

_____26. "You've Never Been This Far Before."

_____27. "Swanee."

_____28. A Bob Seger tune.

_____29. "A Boy Named Sue."

_____30. "The Sidewalks of New York."

A. A song sung on the "PTL Club" TV Show. (*Firestarter*)

B. The songs Needles played in front of the State Theater ("Night Surf")

C. The album Sue Snell listened to the night of the Prom. (*Carrie*)

D. The repertoire of the high school band that played at the Caribou shopping center as the Long Walkers passed by. (*The Long Walk*)

E. The song Jerry played on the jukebox in the truck stop. ("Trucks")

F. The song John heard playing somewhere on the third floor of Central Maine Hospital. ("The Woman in the Room")

G. A song played at the Stillson rally. (*The Dead Zone*)

H. The song playing on the jukebox in the Cavalier while Billy and Chris waited in an upstairs room. (*Carrie*)

I. The song that played on the radio as the man who loved flowers strolled New York City. ("The Man Who Loved Flowers")

J. The music liked by Bellis The Fornit. ("The Ballad of the Flexible Bullet")

K. Treehouse music. ("The Body")

L. The song that played on the clock in the ballroom at the Overlook. (*The Shining*)

M. One of the songs on Christine's playlist. (*Christine*)

N. One of the songs played at Maureen Romano's wedding. ("The Wedding Gig")

O. A song sung on "The Merv Griffin Show." (*Roadwork*)

P. A song played on a honky-tonk piano in Tull. (*The Dark Tower: The Gunslinger*)

Q. One of the songs Stan Soames sang while flying Sam and Naomi to Des Moines. ("The Library Policeman")

R. The song one of the truckers played on the jukebox the night the Prisoner met Nona. ("Nona")

S. Larry Underwood's first (and only) hit single. (*The Stand*)

T. The song Seth Hagstrom and his band were trying to play the night his father discovered the powers of the word processor. ("Word Processor of the Gods")

U. The song the Rangers performed at Dell's. (*'Salem's Lot*)

V. The music played in the Buckeye Mall. (*The Talisman*)

W. A song performed by the Ragged Edge that Donna could hear in the Pinto. (*Cujo*)

X. One of the tapes in Paul Sheldon's car. (*Misery*)

Y. The tune Larry imagined playing on the clock in Central Park. (*The Stand*)

Z. The hymn Tom Cullen sang after he opened his Christmas gifts from Stu. (*The Stand*)

AA. The song Baby Hortense would sing in the tent prayer meetings. ("Children of the Corn")

BB. One of Bobbi's Anderson's favorite groups. (*The Tommyknockers*)

CC. The song the Nazis sang to their children as they fed them poison at the end of the Third Reich. ("Apt Pupil")

DD. A song Mrs. Granger enjoyed singing. (*Rage*)

"MACABRE MOMENTS"

Quiz 43

Macabre. Funereal. Ghastly. Gruesome. Sepulchral. Catch my drift?

The following questions focus on particularly macabre moments from Stephen King's works. Bon Appétit!

1. *Carrie:* How did Tommy Ross die?
2. *'Salem's Lot:* What form of death was as "old as Macedonia," and was something St. Paul and Richard Straker had in common?
3. *Rage:* How did the Cherokees punish their cheating wives?
4. *The Shining:* How did the Donner party survive?
5. *Night Shift:*
   5a. "Jerusalem's Lot": What did James Robert Boone think was in his walls?
   5b. "Graveyard Shift": How did Warwick die?
   5c. "Night Surf": What kind of lighter did Needles use to light Alvin Sackheim's funeral pyre?
   5d. "I am the Doorway": Why did Arthur have hooks instead of hands?
   5e. "The Mangler": What body part did George Stanner lose to the Mangler?
   5f. "The Boogeyman": Where did the Boogeyman hide?
   5g. "Gray Matter": What did Richie Grenadine hide in the wall so he could have it later for lunch?
   5h. "Battleground": How did Renshaw die?

5i. "Trucks": How did the people in the truck stop try and "kill" the renegade bulldozer?

5j. "Sometimes They Come Back": Where did Jim get the blood for his "summoning Wayne" ritual?

5k. "Strawberry Spring": What did Springheel Jack take with him after murdering Ann Bray?

5l. "The Ledge": How long would Norris spend in prison if he was caught with Cressner's heroin in his trunk?

5m. "The Lawnmower Man": What did Alicia Parkette throw up after witnessing the demise of the Smiths' cat?

5n. "Quitters, Inc.": What was step nine in the Quitters, Inc., program?

5o. "I Know What You Need": What was Ed Hamner's "specialty"?

5p. "Children of the Corn": When Vicky was crucified, what was stuffed into her gouged-out eyes?

5q. "The Last Rung on the Ladder": How did Kitty die?

5r. "The Man Who Loved Flowers": What was the man who loved flowers's murder weapon of choice?

5s. "One for the Road": What happened to Richie Messina?

5t. "The Woman in the Room": Who crossed the line from a heavy habit to a lethal dosage?

6. *The Stand: The Complete & Uncut Edition:* How did Mark Braddock die?

7. *The Long Walk:* What was the name of "The World's First Morbid Musical"?

8. *The Dead Zone:* What did Frank Dodd's suicide note say?

9. *Firestarter:* How did the Shop agents convince Vicky McGee to tell them where Charlie was?

10. *Roadwork:* How many sticks of dynamite did Bart use to blow up his house?

11. *Cujo:* In Tad's dream, who wore a black shiny

raincoat and had eyes that were shiny silver coins?

12. *Creepshow:*
12a. "Father's Day": What did Nathan Grantham do with Sylvia's head?
12b. "The Lonesome Death of Jordy Verrill": How did Jordy die?
12c. "The Crate": How did Wilma Die?
12d. "Something to Tide You Over": How many characters in this story died by drowning?
12e. "They're Creeping Up On You": Where did the cockroaches hide?

13. *The Running Man:* True or False: Ben Richards also appeared as a contestant on "Dig Your Grave."

14. *The Dark Tower: The Gunslinger:*
14a. "The Gunslinger": Who claimed to have wept with Mary at Golgotha?
14b. "The Way Station": Where did Hax hang?
14c. "The Oracle and the Mountains": What did Roland see in the trees that overhung the Oracle's altar?
14d. "The Slow Mutants": Who did Jesus raise from the dead?
14e. "The Gunslinger and the Dark Man": What was the first card in Roland's tarot card fortune?

15. *Different Seasons:*
15a. "Rita Hayworth and Shawshank Redemption": Why was the Durham boy locked in solitary confinement for seven years?
15b. "Apt Pupil": Why did Dussander spray his kitchen with Glade?
15c. "The Body": How did Dennis Lachance die?
15d. "The Breathing Method": How was Dr. McCarron thanked for his assistance with the birth of John Stansfield?

16. *Christine:* What did Leigh choke on?
17. *Pet Sematary:* How did Trixie die?

18. *The Talisman* (with Peter Straub): What was the message Jack saw hacked into the door of the Mendocino Room in the Agincourt?

19. *Thinner:* What word was written in blood on Frank Spurton's forehead?

20. *Cycle of the Werewolf:* Who was found headless, disemboweled, and propped against the war memorial?

21. *Skeleton Crew:*

21a. "The Mist": What was the name of the area's resident "necrologist"?

21b. "Here There Be Tygers": What was the name of Charles's classmate who was eaten alive by a tiger?

21c. "The Monkey": How did the Italian ragman die?

21d. "Cain Rose Up": How did Garrish envision Bailey dying?

21e. "Mrs. Todd's Shortcut": How did the Castle Rock textile man die?

21f. "The Jaunt": What were the body parts Victor Carune successfully teleported?

21g. "The Wedding Gig": How many pallbearers did it take to carry Maureen Romano's coffin?

21h. "Paranoid: A Chant" (poem): How did the narrator kill the dog that had the radio cobweb in its nose?

21i. "The Raft": While in Vietnam, what did Randy's friend learn to do with head lice caught off a human scalp?

21j. "Word Processor of the Gods": How did the kid in Waterbury blow up the doghouse?

21k. "The Man Who Would Not Shake Hands": How did the holy man's son die?

21l. "Beachworld": What saved Rand from Excellent Montoya's tranquilizer dart?

21m. "The Reaper's Image": What smell did Spangler think "might arise from the grave of a virginal young girl, forty years dead"?

124

21n. "Nona": What lived inside the ripped-open body of "the girl" Nona showed the Prisoner in the graveyard?

21o. "For Owen" (poem): What is an art?

21p. "Survivor Type": What did Pine consume after he had eaten everything from the groin down?

21q. "Uncle Otto's Truck": How did George McCutcheon die?

21r. "Morning Deliveries (Milkman #1)": What did Spike keep in a mayonnaise jar in his truck?

21s. "Big Wheels: A Tale of the Laundry Game (Milkman #2)": What did Bobby Driscoll want to do to his wife Marcy?

21t. "Gramma": How did Gramma kill Mrs. Harham?

21u. "The Ballad of the Flexible Bullet": How did Sylvia Plath die?

21v. "The Reach": How did Stewie McClelland lose his foot?

22. *It:* On the morning of May 31, 1985, what poured out of the beer taps in Wally's Spa?

23. *The Dark Tower II: The Drawing of the Three:* Where did Dretto and Truman Alexander bury the mick that Balazar shot?

24. *The Eyes of the Dragon:* What was the book of spells bound in?

25. *Misery:* What did Mrs. Soames see?

26. *The Tommyknockers:* What broke John Leandro's shin, crushed his skull, snapped his spine, and left him dead on the road?

27. *The Dark Half:* How did Jack Halstead die?

28. *Four Past Midnight:*

28a. "The Langoliers": What happened to Anne Engle in Brian Engle's dream?

28b. "Secret Window, Secret Garden": How did Bump the cat die?

28c. "The Library Policeman": What did the "Ardelia-thing" use to suck fear out of people's eyes, and what did the fear look like?

28d. "The Sun Dog": How did the man in Bath kill his wife?

29. *The Dark Tower III: The Waste Lands:* What was the disease called that gave Gasher the oozing sores on his face?

30. *Needful Things:* How did Wilma Jerzyck die?

Bonus Question:
"One More Morbid Moment"

Q: What was used to cut off Sneakers's left hand, and what was done with the hand?

Please Allow Me to Introduce Myself . . .

"PLEASE ALLOW ME TO INTRODUCE MYSELF . . ." A Character Biographical Quiz

Quizzes 44–73

The following quizzes test your knowledge of a few biographical facts about thirty important Stephen King characters. (And the characters and questions are in no particular bibliographic or chronological order.) To assist you, the work in which these characters appear is also given, although these people are so well-known in the World of King that you should be able to immediately recognize their name—and their story. The questions about their lives and times are another story—some of them might be a tad tough. But as always, you know exactly where to find the answers—and I don't mean in the back of this book! You can always spend an enjoyable period hunting for the correct response in the actual King work, right? Right!

Quiz 44. "Jack Torrance" (*The Shining*)
        44a. What was the name of Jack's sister?
        44b. What kind of binoculars did Jack own?
        44c. What was the title of the book Jack thought he would write and which would win him the Pulitzer Prize?
        44d. What was the name of Jack Torrance's literary agent?
        44e. How did Jack Torrance die?

Quiz 45. "Carrie White" (*Carrie*)
45a. When was Carrie White born?
45b. What was the name of the Chamberlain department store where Carrie usually bought the material she used to make her clothing?
45c. What was Carrie's body temperature during "flexing"?
45d. What was her blood pressure?
45e. How did Carrie exact revenge for being showered in pig's blood at the Prom?

Quiz 46. "Tad Trenton" (*Cujo*)
46a. What kind of calendar did Tad have hanging in his room?
46b. What was Tad's breakfast in the Pinto?
46c. Who wore a black shiny raincoat and held a stop sign in Tad's dream?
46d. Who was Tad's favorite *Star Wars* guy?
46e. What did Tad call a car's air cleaner?

Quiz 47. "Billy Halleck" (*Thinner*)
47a. What term did Dr. Houston use to describe the "ever-Thinner" Billy Halleck?
47b. In his "pre-curse" days, what was Billy's usual breakfast?
47c. What kind of beer did Billy drink?
47d. What was Billy Halleck's home phone number?
47e. What medical tests did Billy have at the Glassman Clinic?

Quiz 48. "Mother Abagail" (*The Stand* and *The Stand: The Complete & Uncut Edition*)
48a. What was the name of Mother Abagail's father?
48b. What year did Mother Abagail get her first TV set?
48c. Name one of the songs Mother Abagail performed (when she was still Abagail

Trotts) on December 27, 1895, at the Nebraska Grange Hall.

48d. In Mother Abagail's farewell note to the Free Zone, what did she say her sin had been?

48e. What year did Mother Abagail turn 100 years old? (WARNING: TRICK QUESTION!)

Quiz 49. "Ray Garraty" (*The Long Walk*)

49a. What was the name of Ray Garraty's father, and what happened to him?

49b. What happened to Ray when he helped Mr. Elwell take in his hay?

49c. What did Garraty do when he got a charley horse on the road to Augusta?

49d. What Ray Bradbury story did Ray think of when he fell to his knees on the road and a crowd gathered to watch?

49e. Where did Ray Garraty live?

Quiz 50. "Bill Denbrough" (*It*)

50a. What was the name of Bill's wife?

50b. What was Bill Denbrough's "Story Theory"?

50c. What kind of wax did Bill use to waterproof Georgie's newspaper boat?

50d. What was Bill's anti-stuttering (and anti-It) magic sentence?

50e. For the Film Freaks: Who played Bill Denbrough in the 1990 ABC Novel for Television Miniseries version of the novel?

Quiz 51. "Annie Wilkes" (*Misery*)

51a. Where did Annie keep her drug stash?

51b. During the period when Paul was writing *Misery's Return*, how much did Annie owe in back property taxes?

51c. What did Annie drive?

51d. Where did Annie go now and then,

"sometimes to laugh, but mostly to scream"?
51e. What was the date Annie went on trial for the death of Girl Christopher, a one-day-old newborn?

Quiz 52. "Roland LeBay" (*Christine*)
52a. What was the name of Roland's brother?
52b. What was the name of Roland's wife?
52c. When did Roland buy Christine?
52d. How much did Roland pay for Christine?
52e. How old was Roland when he died?

Quiz 53. "David Drayton" ("The Mist")
53a. What did Dave Drayton do for a living?
53b. What was the name of Dave's insurance agent?
53c. What did Dave dub the ten people in the supermarket who absolutely refused to believe that there were monsters in the mist?
53d. What was Dave's college alma mater?
53e. What was the name of the painting Dave once did that showed the Federal Supermarket building and a line of Campbell's Beans and Franks cans in the parking lot?

Quiz 54. "Sunlight Gardener" (*The Talisman*)
54a. What was Sunlight Gardener's real name?
54b. Who was Reverend Gardener's Twinner?
54c. What message was written on the Sunlight Gardener Home's envelopes?
54d. What Psalm did Reverend Gardener read at the first evening prayer service that Jack and Wolf attended at the Sunlight Gardener Home?
54e. What was the name of the magazine published by the Gardener organization?

Quiz 55. "Ardelia Lortz" ("The Library Policeman")
55a. What was the only thing left of the Ardelia-thing after it exploded in the library?
55b. What book did Ardelia suggest to Sam as an aid to writing his Rotary speech?
55c. What Robert McCammon novel had Ardelia had bound in Vinabind?
55d. What was the charge for issuing an adult library card at the "Ardelia Lortz" version of the Junction City Public Library?
55e. What year did Ardelia Lortz kill two children, and then herself?

Quiz 56. "Polly Chalmers" (*Needful Things*)
56a. When Polly left Castle Rock in 1970, whose baby was she carrying?
56b. When Polly was living in San Francisco, what did her one good outfit consist of?
56c. What was the name of Polly's mother?
56d. What was the name of Polly's illegitimate son?
56e. What was the name of Polly's business?

Quiz 57. "Jim Gardener" (*The Tommyknockers*)
57a. What was "Gardener's First Rule for Touring Poets"?
57b. What did Gard think was probably his best poem?
57c. Where did Gard have a skiing accident when he was seventeen?
57d. What was the name of Gard's oft-rejected book of poems about nuclear power?
57e. What type of blood did Gard have?

Quiz 58. "Nick Hopewell" ("The Langoliers")
58a. How old was Nick when he first went through the rip in time?
58b. Before his sacrificial suicide, what did

Nick tell Laurel Stevenson to do after her return trip?

58c. What was Nick's branch of clandestine undercover service?

58d. What was the name of the rich politician whose girlfriend Nick was assigned to "fluff"?

58e. Which of Nick's body parts was Teflon?

Quiz 59. "Kurt Dussander/Arthur Denker" ("Apt Pupil" from *Different Seasons*)

59a. Who was on Dussander's List of Great Murderers from the Past?

59b. What did Dussander spray his kitchen with to get rid of the smell of the cat he had roasted in his oven?

59c. Where was Dussander in 1965?

59d. What was the term used to describe Dussander in an article in *Men's Action* magazine?

59e. What brand of bourbon did Dussander drink?

Quiz 60. "Flagg" (*The Eyes of the Dragon*)

60a. What was the occupation of Bill Hinch, Flagg's manifestation 250 years before King Roland's reign?

60b. What was the closest Flagg could come to being invisible?

60c. What was Flagg's paperweight made of?

60d. What made up the lock on Flagg's triple-locked teak "poison" box?

60e. Flagg cured Anna Crookbows's son of what disease?

Quiz 61. "It/Pennywise/Bob Gray" (*It*)

61a. What was It's "cycle"?

61b. What devastation was It responsible for in Derry between 1929 and 1930?

61c. What afflictions was Richie Tozier threatened with when the Derry Paul Bunyan statue came to life and turned into Pennywise the clown?

61d. What day did It die?

61e. After Bill killed It, what did the Other say?

Quiz 62. "Charlie McGee" (*Firestarter*)

62a. What was Charlie's birthday?

62b. Name one of Charlie's favorite books as a five-year-old.

62c. What was the name of the pond where Charlie used to go fishing with her grandfather?

62d. What was the name of the drug the Shop decided to administer to Charlie while they had her in captivity?

62e. What was the name of the Shop operative who monitored Charlie's cell/room?

Quiz 63. "Marty Coslaw" (*Cycle of the Werewolf*)

63a. How many notes did Marty send Reverend Lowe?

63b. What was the name of Marty's sister?

63c. Which of the beast's eyes did Marty destroy with a firecracker?

63d. What did Marty's third note to Reverend Lowe say?

63e. What was the name of Marty's father?

Quiz 64. "Morton Rainey" ("Secret Window, Secret Garden" from *Four Past Midnight*)

64a. What was the name of the novel Mort wrote that was optioned by Paramount?

64b. What were the two titles Mort bestowed upon his sofa?

64c. What was Mort's Derry address?

64d. How much were the 124 bottles of wine Mort lost in the Derry fire worth?

64e. What kind of typewriter did Mort use before he got the word processor?

Quiz 65. "Jud Crandall" (*Pet Sematary*)
65a. What was the name of Jud's wife?
65b. What was the number of Jud Crandall's cemetery plot?
65c. What was the name of Jud's dog?
65d. What year did Jud's dog die?
65e. What brand of beer did Jud serve at his house?

Quiz 66. "Kurt Barlow" (*'Salem's Lot*)
66a. What were the three nationalities Matt Burke suspected as Barlow's probable origin?
66b. How did Barlow get into the Marsten house?
66c. What items did Matt tell Ben and the others to bring for their confrontation with Barlow?
66d. Who was Barlow's master?
66e. Who wrote *Dracula*?

Quiz 67. "Thad Beaumont" (*The Dark Half*)
67a. What was the name of the pet raccoon Thad had when he was an Appalachian Trail guide?
67b. How many students applied for Thad's honors course in creative writing?
67c. Who was Bill Prebble?
67d. What was the name of Thad's mother?
67e. Who was swimming with Thad the day Thad almost drowned in Lake Davis?

Quiz 68. "Ben Richards" (*The Running Man*)
68a. How much did Ben's room at the Boston Y.M.C.A. cost?
68b. How much did Ben weigh?
68c. What was Ben's certified Weschler Test IQ?

68d. What year did Ben decide to become a contestant on "The Running Man"?

68e. Name one of the three books the bell-boy brought Ben the night before his appearance on "The Running Man."

Quiz 69. "Frank Dodd" (*The Dead Zone*)
69a. What was the name of Frank's mother?
69b. Who was Frank's first murder victim?
69c. Which of Frank's victims was murdered in November of 1974?
69d. Who took a course in Rural Law Enforcement with Frank Dodd at the University of Colorado in the fall of 1972?
69e. What did Frank use to commit suicide?

Quiz 70. "Charlie Decker" (*Rage*)
70a. What was the name of the bully who reminded Charlie of a Briggs & Stratton lawnmower?
70b. Where did Charlie's parents meet?
70c. What was the musical "piece" Charlie thought of every time he heard Bach?
70d. What did Charlie feel emergency vehicles should do as they drove to their destination?
70e. What kind of lighter did Charlie use to set fire to the contents of his locker?

Quiz 71. "Lard Ass Hogan" ("The Revenge of Lard Ass Hogan" from "The Body" from *Different Seasons*)
71a. What was Lard Ass's real name?
71b. What was the name of the butcher at the Freedom Market who weighed the pies every year?
71c. What did Lard Ass drink before the pie-eating contest?
71d. Where was "The Revenge of Lard Ass Hogan" originally published?

71e. For the Film Freaks: Who played Lard Ass Hogan in *Stand By Me*?

Quiz 72. "Reginald 'Pop' Merrill" ("The Sun Dog" from *Four Past Midnight*)

72a. What was Pop's term for the people who believed in an unseen world?

72b. What was the price of the "spirit trumpet" Pop once sold a Mad-Hatter in Dunwich, Massachusetts?

72c. What kind of matches did Pop use to light his pipe?

72d. What kind of car did Pop drive?

72e. How much was the coin collection in Pop's worktable drawer worth?

Quiz 73. "The Tick-Tock Man" (*The Dark Tower III: The Waste Lands*)

73a. What was the color of the Tick-Tock Man's hair?

73b. What did the Tick-Tock Man wear around his neck?

73c. How did the Tick-Tock Man kill the dark-haired woman who laughed too much?

73d. Who was the Tick-Tock man's great-grandfather?

73e. Who took the Tick-Tock Man's pendulum clock and Seiko watch?

Booze, Beasts, Dates, Mates, Kodes, Kritics, Rhymes, & Rods

"THE *PET SEMATARY* BEVY OF BEASTS QUIZ"

Quiz 74

Match either the name of the pet or the name of the owner from the left column with the type of animal he or she was from the right column. (Hint: Five of the pets [not counting the cocker spaniel] are dogs, and two of the pets [not counting the barncats] are cats. Also, there is one "Unknown" pet. This is an animal for whom we are given a name, but no species.)

_____ 1. Hannah
_____ 2. Trixie
_____ 3. Hanratty
_____ 4. Spot
_____ 5. Winston Churchill
_____ 6. Albion Groatley's Animals
_____ 7. Marta
_____ 8. Gen. Patton
_____ 9. Smucky
_____10. Missus Bradleigh's Pet
_____11. Matty Ryder's Pet
_____12. Linda Lavesque's Pet
_____13. Polynesia
_____14. Bowser
_____15. Biffer
_____16. Old Man Fritchie's Birds

A. Dog
B. Raccoon
C. Racing pigeons
D. Bull
E. Rabbit
F. Parakeet
G. Cocker spaniel
H. Parrot
I. Unknown
J. Barncats
K. Cat

"THE KING OF BEERS"

Quiz 75

Stephen King's characters drink. And since Stephen King is who he is, his characters drink *name brand* products. This quiz asks you to match the booze with the boozer, and to help you along, the work in which the drink and the drinker appear is given parenthetically next to the character's name. *Salud!*

_____ 1. Barony Fifth Vat
_____ 2. Miller beer
_____ 3. Jack Daniels
_____ 4. American Grain beer
_____ 5. Rheingold beer
_____ 6. Perrier-Jouet champagne
_____ 7. Busch beer
_____ 8. Apple Zapple wine
_____ 9. Coors beer
_____10. Miller Light Beer
_____11. J.W. Dant whiskey
_____12. Schlitz Light beer
_____13. Coke and Bacardi
_____14. Harp Lager
_____15. Rolling Rock beer
_____16. Irish Mist
_____17. Jim Beam
_____18. Iron City beer
_____19. Digger's Rye
_____20. Budweiser beer
_____21. Black Label beer
_____22. Golden Light beer

_____23. Beck beer
_____24. Gin fizz
_____25. Chivas Regal
_____26. Narragansett beer
_____27. Gin and tonic
_____28. Iron City Light beer
_____29. Cutty Sark. Double. Water back.
_____30. Black Velvet
_____31. Cutty Sark
_____32. Ripple wine
_____33. Lancer's wine
_____34. Clough & Poor gin
_____35. Dixie beer
_____36. VSOP brandy
_____37. Dom Perignon champagne
_____38. Bourbon and bitters
_____39. Ancient Age bourbon
_____40. Brandy
_____41. Glenfiddich scotch
_____42. Olympia beer
_____43. Star whiskey
_____44. Schlitz Light beer
_____45. Gin and prune juice
_____46. Pabst beer
_____47. Gallo wine
_____48. Old Kentucky
_____49. Utica Club beer
_____50. Stroh's beer

A. Stewie McClelland ("The Reach")
B. Billy Halleck (*Thinner*)
C. Andy Dufresne ("Rita Hayworth and Shawshank Redemption")
D. Billy Nolan (*Carrie*)
E. Cary Rossington (*Thinner*)
F. Kurt Dussander ("Apt Pupil")
G. Mrs. Ramage (*Misery's Return*, Version 2; *Misery*)
H. Homer Buckland ("Mrs. Todd's Shortcut")
I. Roger Chatsworth (*The Dead Zone*)

J. Susan Norton (*'Salem's Lot*)

K. Vi Mitla ("The Moving Finger")

L. PC Vetter ("Crouch End")

M. Stan Uris (*It*)

N. Harold Parkette ("The Lawnmower Man")

O. Phyllis Sandler (*The Shining*)

P. The Fair Weather Club (*The Talisman*)

Q. Richard Ginelli (*Thinner*)

R. Jack Slade (*Slade*)

S. Mr. Nordhoff ("Word Processor of the Gods")

T. Roger Breakstone (*Cujo*)

U. Ben Hanscom (*It*)

V. John Renshaw ("Battleground")

W. Richie Grenadine ("Gray Matter")

X. Randy ("The Raft")

Y. Brent Norton ("The Mist")

Z. Louis Creed (*Pet Sematary*)

AA. Kenny Guilder (*Christine*)

BB. Gerard Lumley ("One for the Road")

CC. Roland (*The Dark Tower: The Gunslinger*)

DD. Jud Crandall (*Pet Sematary*)

EE. Eddie Kaspbrak (*It*)

FF. Bobbi Anderson (*The Tommyknockers*)

GG. Jim and Sally Norman ("Sometimes They Come Back")

HH. Henry Wilson ("The Ballad of the Flexible Bullet")

II. Delores Williams ("Dedication")

JJ. Ralph (*Christine*)

KK. Dick Morrison ("Quitters, Inc.")

LL. Bill Hanlon (*It*)

MM. Bill Denbrough (*It*)

NN. David Adley ("The Breathing Method")

OO. Stu Redman (*The Stand*)

PP. Dexter Stanley ("The Crate")

QQ. Mike Hanlon (*It*)

RR. Keenan ("The Fifth Quarter")

SS. Sally Magliore (*Roadwork*)

TT. Irv Manders (*Firestarter*)

"GET YOUR MOTOR RUNNIN' "

Quiz 76

"But at my back from time to time I hear
The sound of horns and motors . . ."
—T. S. Eliot, "The Fire Sermon" (in *The Waste Land*)

"Rolling stock" has always been part of Stephen King's "stock in trade," you know? (Sorry.) This quiz asks you to match the vehicles with the owner or driver. The novel or short story in which the driver and the driven appear is supplied in order to help you track down the right answer.

Onward. (Head out on the highway.)

_____ 1. A Packard coupe
_____ 2. A Corvette
_____ 3. A 1966 Chrysler hardtop
_____ 4. An LTD
_____ 5. A Hudson
_____ 6. A Dodge pickup
_____ 7. A Dodge
_____ 8. A Rolls-Royce Silver Wraith
_____ 9. A Chevy Nova
_____10. A 1977 Plymouth
_____11. An orange Vega
_____12. A Cadillac Coupe de Ville
_____13. A Studebaker
_____14. A Cadillac Cimarron
_____15. A 1952 DeSoto

_____16. A 1948 DeSoto
_____17. A Camaro
_____18. A 1957 Chevrolet pickup
_____19. A Pinto
_____20. A black 1984 Cadillac El Dorado
_____21. A 1960 T-Bird
_____22. A 1975 Duster
_____23. A 1971 Camaro
_____24. A Bangor & Orono Yellow Cab
_____25. A 1956 Buick
_____26. A Mustang
_____27. A white Continental
_____28. A 1957 Pontiac
_____29. A Buick Electra
_____30. A 1966 Imperial
_____31. A gray van
_____32. A Mercedes
_____33. A Chevy Bel Air
_____34. A 1971 Ford Econoline
_____35. A 1976 blue Cadillac
_____36. A Datsun Z
_____37. A 1974 Toyota Corolla
_____38. A blue Camaro
_____39. A 1964 Dodge
_____40. A 1981 Oldsmobile 98
_____41. A beige Chevrolet Caprice
_____42. A Chevrolet Impala Sedan
_____43. A blue Chevy pickup
_____44. A 1952 Chevrolet
_____45. A four-wheel drive Scout
_____46. A 1977 Ford station wagon
_____47. An Opel
_____48. A 1959 Mercury
_____49. A used Buick
_____50. A 1957 Cadillac
_____51. A Mercedes diesel
_____52. A T-Bird
_____53. A 1965 Mercury
_____54. A red Fiat
_____55. A blue Ford

A. The car that Rocket Man was trapped in in Part 6 of the serial (*Misery*)
B. Gary Pervier's car (*Cujo*)
C. Dan Miller's truck ("The Mist")
D. Mr. Tessio's car ("The Body")
E. Mrs. Li-Tsu's car ("Survivor Type")
F. Dennis Guilder's car (*Christine*)
G. The "Trucks" narrator's car ("Trucks")
H. Mrs. Snell's car (*Carrie*)
I. Chuck Spier's car (*The Dead Zone*)
J. Tookey's vehicle ("One for the Road")
K. Amos Culligan's car ("The Monkey")
L. Orville Jamieson's and George Sedaka's car (*Firestarter*)
M. Steve Kemp's van (*Cujo*)
N. Roy Brannigan's car (*The Stand*)
O. Brent Norton's car ("The Mist")
P. The car driven by the man who brought Annie her back tax bill (*Misery*)
Q. The car that killed Jake Chambers (*The Dark Tower: The Gunslinger*)
R. Stan Uris's car (*It*)
S. Richler's car ("Apt Pupil")
T. The car Cape Cod Limousine gave Eddie Kaspbrak for his ride into Derry (*It*)
U. The car in which Adelle Parkins "went to pieces." (Sorry. Couldn't resist.) ("Strawberry Spring")
V. Burt and Vicky's car ("Children of the Corn")
W. Franklin Boddin's truck (*'Salem's Lot*)
X. The car that hit and killed Tony Lombard ("I Know What You Need")
Y. Mr. Pasioco's vehicle (*Firestarter*)
Z. Donna Trenton's car (*Cujo*)
AA. Tony Glick's car (*'Salem's Lot*)
BB. Ophelia Todd's car ("Mrs. Todd's Shortcut")
CC. Ed Hamner,Sr.'s, car ("I Know What You Need")
DD. Ace Merrill's car ("The Body")
EE. Pig Pen's gift from his uncle (*Rage*)

FF. Miss Kinney's boyfriend's car ("Here There Be Tygers")
GG. Ed Hamner's car ("I Know What You Need")
HH. The Devon Woods murder car ("Big Wheels: Tales of the Laundry Game [Milkman #2]")
II. Ellen Hobart's car (*Roadwork*)
JJ. Will Darnell's car (*Christine*)
KK. Larry Underwood's "pre-flu" car (*The Stand*)
LL. Roger Chatsworth's car (*The Dead Zone*)
MM. Ronnie Hanelli's car ("Survivor Type")
NN. The car Halloran rented from Hertz in Colorado (*The Shining*)
OO. Milo Pressman's car ("The Body")
PP. Ray Garraty's mother's car (*The Long Walk*)
QQ. Norman Blanchette's car ("Nona")
RR. Vinnie Mason's new car (*Roadwork*)
SS. Billy Halleck's *adult* car (*Thinner*)
TT. Cap's car (*Firestarter*)
UU. Mrs. Houston's car (*Thinner*)
VV. The vehicle John Smith was riding in when he had his "coma" accident (*The Dead Zone*)
WW. Constable Neary's vehicle (*Cycle of the Werewolf*)
XX. Gorgeous George's car (*The Stand*)
YY. Mike Scollay's car ("The Wedding Gig")
ZZ. Billy Halleck's *first* car (*Thinner*)
AAA. Terry Lennox's car ("The Breathing Method")
BBB. Bart Dawes's car (*Roadwork*)
CCC. The car in which Marty Masen was killed (*Cujo*)

"MARITAL MAYHEM"

Quiz 77

"The most happy marriage I can picture
or imagine to myself would be the union
of a deaf man to a blind woman."
　　—Samuel Taylor Coleridge, from *Recollections*

"My definition of marriage . . . it resembles a pair of
shears, so joined that they cannot be separated;
often moving in opposite directions, yet always
punishing anyone who comes between them."
　　—Rev. Sydney Smith, from *Memoir*

This quiz asks you to match fifty married "Stephen King" couples. The first column contains the first name, surname, and the work in which they appear of one half of a married couple. The second column contains the first name of the spouse. (And, yes, there are two Andys. Either one will be acceptable for the correct spouse!)

_____ 1. Carla Parkette ("The Lawnmower Man")
_____ 2. Rich Jenks (*Carrie*)
_____ 3. Sharon McCann ("Quitters, Inc.")
_____ 4. David Drayton ("The Mist")
_____ 5. Philip Sawyer (*The Talisman*)
_____ 6. Henry Northrup ("The Crate")
_____ 7. Vicky McGee (*Firestarter*)
_____ 8. Ralph McCausland (*The Tommyknockers*)
_____ 9. Bill Flanders ("The Reach")
_____10. Bill Shelburn ("The Monkey")

_____46. Jack Torrance (*The Shining*)
_____47. Gerard Lumley ("One for the Road")
_____48. Linda Dufresne ("Rita Hayworth and Shaw-
           shank Redemption")
_____49. Laura Soames ("The Library Policeman")
_____50. Rebecca Hull ("The Doctor's Case")

A. George	Z. Colette
B. Wilma	AA. Stella
C. Lonnie	BB. Jim
D. Harold	CC. Louis
E. Sandra	DD. Lester
F. Michael	EE. John
G. Richard	FF. Sheila
H. Vera	GG. Donna
I. Milt	HH. Billy
J. Mort	II. Andy
K. Harvey	JJ. Albert
L. Ralph	KK. Francie
M. Bill	LL. Sarah
N. Mark	MM. Vicky
O. Monica	NN. Stan
P. Mary	OO. Wendy
Q. Norman	PP. Rita
R. Cassandra	QQ. Alice
S. William	RR. Marjorie
T. Thad	SS. Rita
U. Reg	TT. Lina
V. Cora	UU. Steffy
W. Ophelia	VV. Bart
X. Jimmy	WW. Andy
Y. Lily Cavanaugh	XX. Ruth

"TALKIN' 'BOUT . . ."

Quiz 78

By 1991, there were more than thirty books written *about* Stephen King. Serious King fans pay attention to these tomes, and many collect and study them. This quiz asks you to match the author/editor with the book he or she has written about Stephen King. (And here's a hint [as if you couldn't tell!]: Some of the authors listed are responsible for more than one title.)

____ 1. Edward J. Zagorski
____ 2. Michael R. Collings
____ 3. Gary Hoppenstand and Ray B. Browne
____ 4. Tim Underwood and Chuck Miller
____ 5. James Van Hise
____ 6. Jeff Conner
____ 7. George Beahm
____ 8. Carroll Terrell
____ 9. Jessie Horsting
____10. David Engebretson
____11. Tony Magistrale
____12. Darrell Schweitzer
____13. Douglas E. Winter
____14. Stephen Spignesi
____15. Don Herron
____16. Joseph Reino
____17. Tyson Blue

A. *The Stephen King Quiz Book*
B. *The Unseen King*
C. *Feast of Fear: Conversations with Stephen King*
D. *Steve King: Man and Artist*

E. *The Stephen King Phenomenon*
F. *Discovering Stephen King*
G. *Teacher's Manual: Novels of Stephen King*
H. *Bare Bones: Conversations on Terror with Stephen King*
I. *Kingdom of Fear: The World of Stephen King*
J. *The Stephen King Companion*
K. *Stephen King Goes to Hollywood*
L. *The Shape Under the Sheet: The Complete Stephen King Encyclopedia*
M. *Enterprise Incidents Presents Stephen King*
N. *The Films of Stephen King*
O. *Stephen King as Richard Bachman*
P. *The Moral Voyages of Stephen King*
Q. *Stephen King: The First Decade,* Carrie *to* Pet Sematary
R. The Shining Reader
S. *Reign of Fear: Fiction and Film of Stephen King*
T. *Stephen King At the Movies*
U. *The Gothic World of Stephen King: Landscape of Nightmares*
V. *The Shorter Works of Stephen King*
W. *Stephen King: The Art of Darkness*
X. *Fear Itself: The Horror Fiction of Stephen King*
Y. *The Many Facets of Stephen King*
Z. *Landscape of Fear: Stephen King's American Gothic*
AA. *The Stephen King Story*

"THE HIDDEN KINGDOM"
A Stephen King Character Fill-in Puzzle

Quiz 79

This quiz is a variation on the old "Word Search" puzzles, but instead of being given a grid with all the words filled in, with this puzzle, you are given a grid with *none* of the words filled in, and asked to put them where they belong. The letters already in the grid are those letters that are not part of any of the names in the Word List.

To assist you in filling in the boxes, for each name, you are given a set of coordinates. These coordinates are for the *first letter* of the name. You will then have to figure out in what direction the names go. The possibilities are forwards, backwards, up, down, or diagonally.

HERB has already been filled in to get you started.

BURT: 11A,14D ("Children of the Corn")
PETER: 8A,11D (*The Eyes of the Dragon*)
CARRIE WHITE: 1A,1D (*Carrie*)
CHARLIE: 9A,2D (*Firestarter*)
CUJO: 3A,7D (*Cujo*)
HERB: 1A,3D (*The Stand: The Complete & Uncut Edition*)
CUTHBERT: 1A,14D (*The Dark Tower*)
HALLECK: 4A,14D (*Thinner*)
FLAGG: 14A,1D (*The Stand*)
WOLF: 5A,13D (*The Talisman*)

151

JACK: 10A,5D (*The Talisman*)
HALL: 8A,8D ("Graveyard Shift")
MADDIE: 14A,13D ("Home Delivery")
BEN MEARS: 14A,12D (*'Salem's Lot*)
McCARRON: 1A,13D ("The Breathing Method")
TONY: 11A,9D (*The Shining*)
NONA: 5A,6D ("Nona")
CHRISTINE: 1A,1D (*Christine*)
RANDY: 3A,1D ("The Raft")
ANDERS: 12A,1D (*The Talisman*)
STEFF: 14A,5D ("The Mist")
RACKNE: 9A,6D ("The Ballad of the Flexible Bullet")
TODD: 6A,1D ("Apt Pupil")
BROWER: 10A,4D ("The Body")
TRASHCAN MAN: 3A,2D (*The Stand*)

DOWN

ACROSS

	1	2	3	4	5	6	7	8	9	10	11	12	13	14
1		L	H	B	Y									
2			E	R	H	X	V	S	Q	S	B	F	Q	
3			R										J	
4			B		S	R								
5		O		I			O							
6					R					Z	N	Y		
7			G	H		L				N	R		R	
8		O		X			O			L			S	
9										I				
10		B	N				R	A	V					
11		B	H	Q	C	U		U		S				O
12							V			V				S
13		Y	A	I	V	E	Z	U		S	S			N
14							D	W	N		W			O

152

"KING KODES"

Quiz 80

This quiz contains coded quotations from the works of Stephen King. The *same master code key* is used for all ten quotations, so if you can figure out one, you can probably jump all over the others. (And here's a hint: The code key isn't a difficult one. In fact, once you figure it out, you'll probably be able to decode the quotations backwards, forwards, or even in your sleep!) Also, the quotations are all fairly well-known bits of dialogue from King's tales.

1. "SR-BL HROEVI, ZDZBBBBB!"
2. "R PMLD DSZG BLF MVVW"
3. "OVG'H GZMP, BLF ZMW R. OVG'H GZMP ZYLFG UVZI."
4. "WL BLF OLEV?"
5. "IVWIFN"
6. "BVIIIMMM FNYVI DSFMMMM UZBFMMMM"
7. "GSVA UOLZG"
8. "HSLLGRMT HGZIH LMOB"
9. "R'N PRMT LU HSV DLIOW!"
10. "HZOOB"

153

"SAY WHEN?"

Quiz 81

Match the Stephen King work with the year it was published.

___ 1.	*The Tommyknockers*	A. 1989
		B. 1987
___ 2.	*Carrie*	C. 1986
___ 3.	*Creepshow*	D. 1977
___ 4.	*Firestarter*	E. 1981
___ 5.	*Four Past Midnight*	F. 1990
		G. 1978
___ 6.	*Danse Macabre*	H. 1983
___ 7.	*Needful Things*	I. 1984
___ 8.	*Pet Sematary*	J. 1974
___ 9.	*Night Shift*	K. 1982
___10.	*'Salem's Lot*	L. 1980
___11.	*It*	M. 1985
___12.	*The Stand: The Complete & Uncut Edition*	N. 1975
		O. 1991
___13.	*The Shining*	
___14.	*The Talisman*	
___15.	*Skeleton Crew*	
___16.	*Misery*	
___17.	*The Dark Half*	
___18.	*The Eyes of the Dragon*	
___19.	*Christine*	
___20.	*Thinner*	

"PUT IT IN ITS PLACE"

Quiz 82

Think you're a Stephen King fan, huh? Well, then this should be a fairly simple quiz. You do know your King collections, now *don't you*?

This quiz asks you to match the short story or novella from the left column with the King collection in which it appears from the right column. (And you don't have to be Einstein on the beach to figure out that the majority of story titles are going to be from either *Night Shift* or *Skeleton Crew*, right?)

If you can't place a title, try and get as many as you can. But if you're *really* stuck, then I guess we'll have to consider this an "open book" quiz and let you use the Tables of Contents in each of the King collections. But if I know my King fans, I doubt that that will be necessary! Good Luck!

＿＿ 1.	"Uncle Otto's Truck"	A. *Skeleton Crew*
＿＿ 2.	"Something to Tide You Over"	B. *Different Seasons*
＿＿ 3.	"The Woman in the Room"	C. *The Dark Tower: The Gunslinger*
＿＿ 4.	"The Wedding Gig"	D. *Night Shift*
＿＿ 5.	"The Library Policeman"	E. *Four Past Midnight*
＿＿ 6.	"Survivor Type"	F. *Creepshow*
＿＿ 7.	"The Lawnmower Man"	
＿＿ 8.	"Gramma"	

"RHYME THYME"

Quiz 83

This quiz offers six verse excerpts from Stephen King's works. There is poetry here, a song lyric, and even just a random list of images. Your task is to identify the author (or performer, in one case) of the lyric and give details on its origin.

1. "Jesus watches from the wall
   But his face is cold as stone,
   And if he loves me
   As she tells me
   Why do I feel so all alone?"

2. "I know I didn't say I was comin down,
   I know you didn't know I was here in town,
   But bay-yay-yaby you can tell me if anyone can,
   Baby, can you dig your man?
   He's a righteous man,
   Tell me baby, can you dig your man?"

3. "Your hair is winter fire
   January embers
   My heart burns there, too."

4. "These streets begin where the cobbles
   surface through tar like the heads
   of children buried badly in their textures."

5. "ivory guillotine Kowloon
   twisted woman of shadows, like a pig
   some big house"

6. My girl's a corker, she's a New Yorker,
   I buy her everything to keep her in style,
   She got a pair of hips
   Just like two battleships,
   Oh, boy, that's how my money goes."

"AUTHOR, AUTHOR!"—PART 1

· Quiz 84

Many of Stephen King's characters are involved in the creative arts, and this quiz asks you to match the artistic work from the left column with the King character responsible for it from the right column. (There are novels, short stories, books of poetry, nonfiction essays, plays, and paintings included in the list of art works, and some artists are responsible for more than one title.)

This quiz is in two parts. Part 1 will be relatively simple for most fair to middling King fans. Part 2 is considerably more difficult and will likely entail some archaeological work.

_____ 1. *The Buffalo Soldiers*

_____ 2. "The Revenge of Lard Ass Hogan"

_____ 3. "Secret Window, Secret Garden"

_____ 4. "Misery's Hobby"

_____ 5. *The Black Rapids*

_____ 6. "We Survived the Black Prom"

_____ 7. "The Monster Words"

_____ 8. *Strange Resort, The Story of the Overlook Hotel*

_____ 9. "The Blue Air Compressor"

_____10. "The Dark"

_____11. *A History of Old Derry*

_____12. *Book of Spells*

_____13. *My Name Is Susan Snell*

_____14. "Baby, Can You Dig Your Man?"

_____15. *Misery's Quest*

_____16. *The Politics of the Jaunt*

A. Gerald Nately, "The Blue Air Compressor"
B. Branson Buddinger, *It*
C. Jack Torrance, *The Shining*
D. C. K. Summers, "The Jaunt," *Skeleton Crew*
E. Mike Hanlon, *It*
F. Gordon Lachance, "The Body," *Different Seasons*
G. Thad Beaumont & George Stark, *The Dark Half*
H. Bill Denbrough, *It*
I. Vic Trenton, *Cujo*
J. Norma Watson, *Carrie*
K. Alhazred, *The Eyes of the Dragon*
L. Larry Underwood, *The Stand*
M. George Stark, *The Dark Half*
N. Susan Snell, *Carrie*
O. John Shooter, "Secret Window, Secret Garden," *Four Past Midnight*
P. Paul Sheldon, *Misery*
Q. Bobbi Anderson, *The Tommyknockers*

"Author, Author!"—Part 2

Quiz 85

This is the second part of the "Author, Author!" quiz, this part being more difficult.

As in Part 1, this quiz asks you to match the artistic work from the left column with the King character responsible for it from the right column. (There are novels, short stories, books of poetry, nonfiction essays, plays, and paintings included in the list of art works, and, again, some artists are responsible for more than one title.)

_____ 1. "Negative Environmental Factors in Long-Term Animal Migration"
_____ 2. "Did Jesus Have a Dog?"
_____ 3. *These Were Our Brothers*
_____ 4. *A Practical Guide to Pregnancy and Delivery*
_____ 5. *Rimfire Christmas*
_____ 6. "Concerning the Black Holes"
_____ 7. *Chasing Sundown*
_____ 8. "Beans and False Perspective"
_____ 9. "The Spring of the Lord's Love"
_____10. *The Radiation Cycle*
_____11. "Outside Marty's House"
_____12. "Haiku"
_____13. "Crowfoot Mile"
_____14. *The Sleeping Madonna*
_____15. "Diving in the Dirt"
_____16. *True Tales of Demon Infestations*
_____17. *Boys in the Mist*
_____18. *Everybody Drops the Dime*

A. Steve Kemp, *Cujo*
B. Ben Hanscom, *It*
C. Bobbi Anderson, *The Tommyknockers*
D. David Drayton, "The Mist," *Skeleton Crew*
E. Mrs. Guilder, *Christine*
F. Rev. Lester Lowe, *Cycle of the Werewolf*
G. Ben Mears, *'Salem's Lot*
H. Hank Olson, *The Long Walk*
I. George Stark, *The Dark Half*
J. Reg Thorpe, "The Ballad of the Flexible Bullet," *Skeleton Crew*
K. Edward Gray Seville, "The Breathing Method," *Different Seasons*
L. Jim Gardener, *The Tommyknockers*
M. Peter Jefferies, "Dedication"
N. Morton Rainey, "Secret Window, Secret Garden," *Four Past Midnight*
O. Peter Rosewall, "Dedication"
P. The Dead Beats, "Sneakers"
Q. Carlos Detweiller, *The Plant*
R. John and Elise Graham, "Rainy Season"
S. John Kintner, "Secret Window, Secret Garden," *Four Past Midnight*
T. Phyllis Myers, *The Dark Half*
U. Robert Jenkins, "The Langoliers," *Four Past Midnight*

V. Jack Torrance, *The Shining*

W. Larry Underwood, *The Stand*

X. Dr. Emlyn McCarron, "The Breathing Method," *Different Seasons*

Y. Thad Beaumont, *The Dark Half*

Z. Charlie Gereson, "The Crate" (*Gallery* text version)

AA. Gordon Lachance, "The Body," *Different Seasons*)

BB. David Drayton, "The Mist," *Skeleton Crew*

"THIS IS DEDICATED TO . . ."

Quiz 86

Do you ever read the author's dedications in books? I've found that a lot of people do, and that reading them gives a little added insight into the authors' lives. Over the years, I've learned that the more you know about Stephen King's life and work, the easier it is to recognize certain important people and colleagues in his dedications. Stephen King does not dedicate his works frivolously, and thus this quiz takes a look at the people he *has* so honored.

Identify the Stephen King works containing the following dedications.

1. This is for Stephanie and Jim Leonard,
   who know why.
   Boy, *do* they.
2. For Naomi Rachel King
   ". . . promises to keep."
3. For Tabitha King
   ". . . promises to keep."
4.   To
   Ed Ferman
   who took a chance on these stories,
   one by one.
5. For Susan Artz
   and WGT
6. For my wife Tabitha:
   This dark chest of wonders.
7. In memory of Davis Grubb,
   and all the voices of Glory.
8. This is in memory

of John D.
MacDonald. I miss
you, old friend
—and you were
right about the
tigers.

9. It's easy enough—perhaps too easy—to memorial-
ize the dead. This book is for six great writers
of the macabre who are still alive.

ROBERT BLOCH
JORGE LUIS BORGES
RAY BRADBURY
FRANK BELKNAP LONG
DONALD WANDREI
MANLY WADE WELLMAN

———

*Enter, Stranger, at your Riske: Here there be
Tygers.*

10. For Russ and Florence Dorr

11. This is for Joe Hill King, who shines on.

12. This is for George Romero and
Chris Forrest Romero.
And the Burg.

13. This book is for
Arthur and Joyce Greene

14. This is for
Chuck Verrill

15. FOR TABBY
this dark chest of wonders.

16. This book is for Shirley Sonderegger
who helps me mind my business,
and for her husband, Peter.

17. This book is for
RUTH KING
ELVENA STRAUB

18. In memory of Shirley Jackson
who never needed to raise her voice.
The Haunting of Hill House
The Lottery

The Lottery
We Have Always Lived in the Castle
The Sundial

19. In memory of Charlotte Littlefield.
    Proverbs 31:10–28.
20. For Kirby McCauley
21. To Don Grant, who's taken a chance on these
    novels, one by one.
22. THIS IS FOR OWEN
    I LOVE YOU, OLD BEAR
23. This story is for my great friend BEN STRAUB,
    and for my daughter, NAOMI KING.
24. This is for Joe,
    another white-
    knuckle flier.
25. For Peter and Susan Straub
26. This is for Tabby, who got me into it—
    and then bailed me out of it.
27. This book is gratefully dedicated to my children.
    My mother and my wife taught me how to be
    a man. My children taught me how to be free.
       NAOMI RACHEL KING, at fourteen;
       JOSEPH HILLSTROM KING, at twelve;
       OWEN PHILIP KING, at seven.
    Kids, fiction is the truth inside the lie, and the
    truth of this fiction is simple enough: *the magic
    exists*.
28.   This is for Jim Bishop
       and Burt Hatlen and Ted Holmes.
29. This is for the
    staff and
    patrons of the
    Pasadena Public
    Library.
30. For Elaine Koster and Herbert Schnall

"CHAPTER BY CHAPTER"

Quiz 87

Match the Stephen King chapter or book subdivision titles in the left column with the work in which they appear from the right column. (Fifty chapter or division titles are given, all taken from a total of twenty-seven works.)

_____ 1. "Interoffice Memo"

_____ 2. "Fall from Innocence"

_____ 3. "The Coming of the Sparrows"

_____ 4. "The Ritual of Chüd"

_____ 5. "Oz the Gweat and Tewwible"

_____ 6. "Purpurfargade Ansiktet"

_____ 7. "What Happened to the Bag-Boy"

_____ 8. "Minus 16 and COUNTING . . ."

_____ 9. "Charlie Alone"

_____10. "A Winter's Tale"

_____11. "The Laughing Tiger"

_____12. "It Was Her!"

_____13. "The Emperor of Ice Cream"

_____14. "The Rabbit"

_____15. "Prom Night"

_____16. "The Betrayal"

_____17. "Going Down the Road"

_____18. "Six Phone Calls"

A. _The Stand: The Complete & Uncut Edition_

B. _Carrie_

C. _Misery_

D. _The Dark Half_

E. _It_

F. _Cycle of the Werewolf_

G. _Firestarter_

H. _Roadwork_

I. _Christine_

J. _The Shining_

K. _The Long Walk_

L. _The Stand_

M. "The Breathing Method," _Different Seasons_

N. _'Salem's Lot_

O. _The Talisman_

P. _Thinner_

"No Limits"

Quiz 88

Stephen King's works are often published in limited editions in addition to their trade editions. These limiteds are usually signed and numbered, slipcased, contain special artwork, and are usually quite beautiful.

Match the King work in the left column with the publishing company responsible for the limited edition of that work in the right column. (Hint: One publisher is responsible for four titles on the list, and another publisher is reponsible for two.)

_____ 1. *Christine*

_____ 2. *It*

_____ 3. *Cycle of the Werewolf*

_____ 4. *The Eyes of the Dragon*

_____ 5. *The Plant*

_____ 6. *Cujo*

_____ 7. *The Dark Tower II: The Drawing of the Three*

_____ 8. *Danse Macabre*

_____ 9. *Dolan's Cadillac*

_____10. *Skeleton Crew*

_____11. *The Stand: The Complete & Uncut Edition*

_____12. *My Pretty Pony*

A. Edition Phantasia
B. Donald M. Grant, Publisher
C. Philtrum Press
D. Doubleday
E. Whitney Museum of American Art
F. Scream Press
G. Lord John Press
H. Mysterious Press
I. Everest House
J. Land of Enchantment
K. Phantasia Press

_____13. *The Talisman*
_____14. *Firestarter*
_____15. *The Dark
Tower: The
Gunslinger*

A Truly *"No Limits"* Bonus Section

Interest in Stephen King and his work is so intense that often even books *about* King and his work appear in limited editions. This quiz tests your knowledge of this particular spoke of the Stephen King "wheel."

Match the book about King in the left column with the company that published the limited edition of that book in the right column.

_____1. *Kingdom of Fear*
_____2. *The Shape Under
the Sheet: The
Complete Stephen
King
Encyclopedia*
_____3. *The Stephen King
Companion*
_____4. *Bare Bones*
_____5. *The Stephen King
Story*

A. The Overlook Connection Press
B. GB Publishing
C. Underwood-Miller

"AKA ..."

It isn't uncommon for writers to use a "working title" when they're in the middle of a project and then change it before publication.

Match Stephen King's original title from the left column with the work as it was eventually titled for publication in the right column.

____1. *Getting It On*   A. *The Shining*
____2. "Time in a Glass   B. "Sometimes They
      That Ran"   Come Back"
____3. *The Shine*   C. *'Salem's Lot*
____4. "And Sometimes   D. "The Woman in the
      They Come Back"   Room"
____5. *Second Coming*   E. *Rage*

"STEVIE'S GOT A GUN"

Quiz 90

"Come my tan-faced children,
Follow well in order, get your weapons ready,
Have you your pistols? have you your sharp-edged
     axes?
Pioneers! O pioneers!"
—Walt Whitman, from *Pioneers! O Pioneers!*

This quiz asks you to match the firearm with the fire-armed. As an aid to the solving, the novel or story from which the character and weapon were taken is also supplied. Shoot 'em up, baby.

_____ 1. A Remington .30-.06
_____ 2. A Smith & Wesson .38
_____ 3. A Winchester
_____ 4. A .22 caliber target pistol
_____ 5. Steyr-Aug semi-automatic machine guns
_____ 6. A Kalishnikov AK-47 assault rifle
_____ 7. A .45 auto
_____ 8. A Spanish Llama .38
_____ 9. A .460 Weatherbee rifle
_____10. A Daisy air rifle
_____11. A shotgun
_____12. A Llama .25
_____13. A .32 caliber revolver
_____14. A .30–.30
_____15. A .45 caliber hogleg
_____16. A Winchester .30–.30
_____17. A .352 Magnum hunting rifle

_____18. A .45 Colt

_____19. A .44 Magnum

_____20. Two .38s, three .45s, a .357 Magnum, six shotguns, and a Schmeisser submachine gun

_____21. Two revolvers

_____22. A .243 caliber Remington 700 rifle

_____23. A Sten gun

_____24. A .38 caliber Colt Woodsman

_____25. A .38 caliber police special

_____26. A Magnum/Springstun

_____27. A loaded .45

_____28. A Weatherbee .360 rifle

_____29. A .357 Magnum

_____30. A Winchester .30–.06

A. Ruth McCausland's shotgun (*The Tommyknockers*)

B. Tony's gun ("The Ledge")

C. The guns used by Jack Rangely, Tony Westerman, and Rollick (*Steel Machine; The Dark Half*)

D. The machine pistol Donahue pointed at McCone on the plane Ben had commandeered (*The Running Man*)

E. Tom Rogan's gun (*It*)

F. The gun Dud Rogers used to kill rats at the dump (*'Salem's Lot*)

G. Sunlight Gardener's gun (*The Talisman*)

H. The weapon John Smith chose with which to assassinate Greg Stillson (*The Dead Zone*)

I. Dave Roberts's gun (*The Stand*)

J. Jack Torrance's gun (*The Shining*)

K. Todd Bowden's "shooting spree" gun ("Apt Pupil")

L. Garrish's "sniper" gun ("Cain Rose Up")

M. The weapon Reg Thorpe bought ("The Ballad of the Flexible Bullet")

N. Harold Lauder's gun (*The Stand*)

O. The gun with which Arthur planned on shooting himself ("I Am the Doorway")

P. Roland's guns (*The Dark Tower: The Gunslinger*)

Q. Henry Parmalee's gun ("Gray Matter")

R. Gary Pervier's gun (*Cujo*)

S. Poke and Lloyd's guns (*The Stand*)

T. The weapon used by the South City police (*The Running Man*)

U. One of the guns Ollie Weeks used for target shooting ("The Mist")

V. A weapon delivered to Ginelli (*Thinner*)

W. Jack Sawyer's childhood gun (*The Talisman*)

X. Rita Blakemoor's gun (*The Stand*)

Y. Bobby Terry's gun (*The Stand*)

Z. The rifle Larry Underwood carried out of New York City (*The Stand*)

AA. One of the guns Bart Dawes bought at Harvey's Gun Shop (*Roadwork*)

BB. The gun that Uncle Al gave to Marty on New Year's Eve (*Cycle of the Werewolf*)

CC. Dirty Harry's gun (*The Dead Zone*)

VII

CELEBRITY GUEST QUIZMASTERS

"ROCKIN' IN THE KING ZONE": A "CASTLE ROCK" QUIZ
by
Tyson Blue*

Quiz 91

Introduction by Stephen Spignesi

Tyson Blue was a contributing editor to the late, great *Castle Rock: The Stephen King Newsletter,* and is also the author of *The Unseen King* and *Notes from the Terminator.*

Tyson is one of those guys for whom the word *expert* was made up: He has spent years studying Stephen King and his work, and it is with great pleasure that I feature him here in these pages.

Tyson's contribution is a (what else?) "Castle Rock" quiz.

I now turn you over to the capable hands of the Blue Man.

Tyson Blue's "Castle Rock" Quiz

So, you think you know your way around Castle Rock, Maine, do you? Well, here's your chance to show it, by matching the residents listed below with the places they're associated with in Stephen King's "Castle Rock" stories. Here's a hint: several names

*©1991 by Tyson Blue

are linked with the same place, and some names are associated with more than one, but everybody has at least one.

_____ 1. Ace Merrill
_____ 2. Gary Pervier
_____ 3. Frank Dodd
_____ 4. Arnold Herbert
_____ 5. Joe Camber
_____ 6. Roger Breakstone
_____ 7. Francine Tupper
_____ 8. George Bannerman
_____ 9. Pop Merrill
_____10. Leland Gaunt
_____11. Polly Chalmers
_____12. John Smith
_____13. Teddy Duchamp
_____14. Alma Frechette
_____15. Ray Brower
_____16. Alan Pangborn
_____17. Molly Durham
_____18. Gordon Lachance
_____19. John Delevan
_____20. Milo Pressman

A. You Sew 'N' Sew
B. The Mellow Tiger
C. Ad Worx
D. The Blue Point Diner
E. Needful Things
F. The Castle County Sheriff's Department
G. Castle Acres Nursing Home
H. The Emporium Galorium
I. Joe Camber's Garage
J. The Coffee Pot
K. Castle Rock Western Auto
L. His house
M. Sukey's Tavern
N. Castle Rock Dump
O. Laverdiere's Super Drug Store
P. Oxford Mills
Q. Castle River Trestle
R. Back Harlow Road
S. Castle Rock High School
T. Gem Theater

"ATTACK OF THE KILLER QUOTES"
by
Stanley Wiater*

Quiz 92

Introduction by Stephen Spignesi

Stanley Wiater is a close friend of mine who also happens to be one of the preeminent practitioners of contemporary horror, fantasy, and science fiction criticism. (See my features on his two seminal collections of interviews, *Dark Dreamers* and *Dark Visions* in the Bibliography.) Stanley also writes (superb) fiction and possesses an almost encyclopedic knowledge of the genre.

This quiz evidences Stanley's wonderfully encompassing awareness of not only the horror field, but of Stephen King and his work as well. I knew Stephen King blurbed other writers' books, but I turned to Stanley Wiater to tell me how many he's blurbed, how often he's blurbed, and what he said while blurbing. (Blurbs, for those of you unfamiliar with book publishing lingo, are brief, complimentary comments by someone respected in the field about another author's work. The quotes are usually placed conspicuously on the front and/or back cover.)

Stanley kindly consented to participate in *The Sec-*

*©1991 by Stanley Wiater

ond Stephen King Quiz Book by contributing the following quiz, which is a sampling of ten of Stanley's favorite King blurbs.

I think you'll find some surprises here . . . and I also think you're going to be hunting down some of the titles mentioned in this quiz that you may have not read.

Match the Stephen King blurb from the left column with the work he blurbed from the column on the right.

_____ 1. "Perhaps the finest psychological horror writer working today . . . and never in finer form."

_____ 2. "May be the scariest haunted house novel ever written."

_____ 3. "America's premier novelist of terror. Nobody does it better."

_____ 4. "The terror just mounts and mounts."

_____ 5. "Terrifying. Her picture of women going slowly mad in a convent during one of history's darkest periods is both gruesome and irresistible."

_____ 6. "One of the premier horror writers of his or any generation."

_____ 7. "The best countdown-to-nuclear-war novel since *Seven Days in May* . . . for my money, a little better."

_____ 8. "Never—never in my life have I been so completely shaken by a collection of stories. I have never experienced such a combination of revulsion, delight, and amazement."

_____ 9. "Like the best popular fiction, the book simply comes at you, finally leaving you shaken and sober and afraid on a deeper level than simple 'thrills' alone furnish."

_____10. "The climax is one of the most effective sequences in modern horror fiction."

A. *Red Dragon* by Thomas Harris
B. *The Doll Who Ate His Mother* by Ramsey Campbell

C. *The Gold Crew* by Thomas Scortia and Frank M. Robinson
D. *The Inhuman Condition* by Clive Barker
E. *Hell House* by Richard Matheson
F. *A Mortal Glamour* by Chelsea Quinn Yarbro
G. *Psycho II* by Robert Bloch
H. *Ghost Story* by Peter Straub
I. *Catacombs* by John Farris
J. *Night Songs* by Charles L. Grant

"NICKED IN THE BUD: NICKNAMES, NASTY AND NICE"
by
Dave Lowell*

Quiz 93

Introduction by Stephen Spignesi

This quiz is part of our Celebrity Guest Quizmasters selection, and our guest Quizmaster today is Dave Lowell, who hails from the Land of the King, Maine.

Dave is a novelist (manuscripts making the rounds of agents and publishers as we speak) and an autograph dealer who was a big help to me when I was putting together my Stephen King encyclopedia, *The Shape Under the Sheet*. Dave was my emissary to Steve's brother Dave King, and Mr. Lowell also contributed photos, antique postcards, and a whole bunch of other good stuff to *The Shape*. (Also, Dave has the singular [dual?] distinction [along with Larry Fire] of being one half of the two-man team that picked up Stephen King—literally—one July afternoon at his office. Dave, Larry, and Dave and Laurie Hinchberger of The Overlook Connection stopped by King's office on their way to NECON to get some books signed, and while there, asked King if they could have a picture with him. Steve-o said, "Sure," and when they went outside, said, "Well, what are you waiting for?

*©1991 by Dave Lowell

Pick me up!" And so they did. Dave Hinchberger shot the picture, and it was published for the first time [in a book] in *The Shape Under the Sheet*.)

Dave's contribution to this Quiz Book is a quiz on the nicknames of King characters. Some of the "nicks" are easy; and some ain't! But I'm sure all you King experts out there can nick this one in the bud! Right? Right!

1. What was the Torrances' nickname for their son Danny?
2. What was Davey Hogan's nickname?
3. What did Arnie Cunningham call the bullies who gave him grief?
4. What did Annie Wilkes call people she was not too fond of?
5. What did Jordy Verrill call himself when he felt he did something wrong or stupid?
6. What was the nickname for the Hadley-Watson Model-6 Speed Ironer and Folder?
7. What did Danny Torrance call his imaginary friend?
8. In *It*, what did the kids call the special group they belonged to?
9. What was Tad Trenton's protective talismanic poem called?
10. What does Stephen King call the ten most used "fears" in horror?

"STUCK IN THE MIDDLE WITH YOU": A MIDDLE NAME QUIZ by Ray Rexer*

Quiz 94

Introduction by Stephen Spignesi

The late Ray Rexer, one of our Celebrity Guest Quizmasters, was a Stephen King fan of the highest order. He was the creator and publisher of *Castle Schlock: The Stephen King Parody Newsletter*, and was also a contributor to my book, *The Shape Under the Sheet: The Complete Stephen King Encyclopedia*.

Ray loved quizzes, puzzles, and games. You might say that Ray was "Raysed" on quizzes. (But then again, you might not.) He had a legendary sense of humor, and I am proud to also feature Ray in this volume.

This quiz originally appeared in the February 1989 issue of *Castle Rock: The Stephen King Newsletter*, and it appears here thanks to the kindness and support of Ray's widow, Elyce.

Ray Rexer's "Middle Name" Quiz

Match the Stephen King character from the left column with his middle name from the right column. Score five points for each correct answer to names 1–

*©1989 by Ray Rexer and Elyce Rexer

10; score twenty-five points for each correct answer to names 11 and 12. The grading system is as follows:

100 points:	CHEATER
60–95 points:	APT PUPIL
26–60 points:	REPLOID
0–25 points:	MALIGNED FORNIT

CHARACTER	MIDDLE NAME
____ 1. Jack Torrance	A. Luther
____ 2. Danny Torrance	B. Paul
____ 3. Greg Stillson	C. No middle name
____ 4. Glen Bateman	D. Anthony
____ 5. Morgan Sloat	E. Edwin
____ 6. Donald Elbert	F. Pequod
____ 7. Johnny Smith	G. Daniel
____ 8. Harold Lauder	H. Ammas
____ 9. George Denbrough	I. Elmer
____ 10. Hubert Marsten	J. Emery
____ 11. Ray Rexer	K. Barclay
____ 12. Stephen King	L. Merwin

VIII

INTRIGUING
INTERROGATORIES:
A
KILLER KING
KROSS-
EXAMINATION

"WHO ARE WE?"
(This Be Tough.)

Quiz 95

This test concerns itself with something interesting and enigmatic about twenty-three Stephen King characters (from fourteen Stephen King works), and it involves deductive reasoning. The questioning is in four parts.

Here's the skinny:

First, you must read through the following brief biographical entries for each character.

Then, answer—in sequential order—the questions that follow the entries.

CARRIE

•ROGER FEARON Roger had worked at Chamberlain Mills and Weaving for eighteen years, but wanted to move out of the Chamberlain area.

THE STAND

•RICHARD FARRIS Farris was the seventy-year-old judge who joined Larry Underwood's group in Joliet, Illinois. He eventually left the Free Zone and, on his way to Las Vegas as a spy for the good guys, was murdered by two of Flagg's men.

•RANDALL FLAGG The Dark Man; the Man with No Face; the Walkin' Dude.

•RAY FLOWERS Ray was the emcee of "Speak Your Piece," the highest-rated morning radio program in Springfield, Missouri.

•RAMSEY FORREST Randall Flagg's alias in Georgia.

•ROBERT FRANQ Randall Flagg's alias in New York.
•RICHARD FRY One of Randall Flagg's aliases.

THE STAND: THE COMPLETE
& UNCUT EDITION
•RUSSELL FARADAY Randall Flagg's reincarnation in the jungle.
•RICHARD FREEMANTLE One of Randall Flagg's aliases.
•ROBERT FREEMONT One of Randall Flagg's aliases.
•RICHARD FRYE One of Randall Flagg's aliases.

THE LONG WALK
•ROGER FENUM Roger was a Long Walker. His number was 13 and he was the fiftieth boy to go down.

THE DEAD ZONE
•ROSCOE FISHER Roscoe was one of Sheriff Bannerman's deputies.

FIRESTARTER
•RICHARD FOLSOM Major Puckeridge's Shop aide.

THINNER
•RAND FOXWORTH Fairview's assistant chief of police.

"CAIN ROSE UP"
•RON FRANE One of the residents of Garrish's dorm.

"THE JAUNT"
•RUDY FOGGIA The convicted murderer who agreed to go through Jaunting awake in exchange for a complete pardon if he came through all right. He didn't come through all right. He emerged insane, and said, "It's eternity in there" before he died of a massive heart attack.

•RAYMOND FOGARTY The minister of the First Methodist Church of Derry. Fogarty presided over Georgie Denbrough's burial rites.
•RALPH FOSTER Bill Denbrough's hand-wrestling opponent.

"THE LIBRARY POLICEMAN"
•RUSS FRAME Russ was a physicians' assistant in Dr. Melden's office.

"CROUCH END"
•ROBERT FARNHAM One of the Crouch End Station cops. He was lost in Crouch End while looking for Lonnie Freeman.

"THE END OF THE WHOLE MESS"
•RICHARD FORNOY Howard and Bobby's father. He was a history major who became a full professor at Hofstra at the age of thirty.

THE DARK TOWER III: THE WASTE LANDS
•RICHARD FANNIN The Ageless Stranger; Maerlyn; Merlin. The dark Wizard who appeared beneath Lud to the Tick-Tock Man after Jake was rescued by Roland. Ticky's "entire consciousness . . . fused into one thought: *I must get away from this beast that looks like a man.*" Fannin remembered an "old acquaintance" who was fond of saying, "My life for you."

Questions

A. The twenty-three characters all have something in common. This common factor is blatant, and should be immediately recognizable. The first part of this question, then, is what do the twenty-three characters have in common?

B. The second part of this question involves making a value judgment about each character. Each character can be "graded" as either falling into one category or another. The criterion for these categories is the simplest of all standards; it is something intrinsic to the nature of horror fiction, and it is something that is instantly recognizable about each character. The second part of this question, then, asks you to first, define the criterion by which you will segregate the characters, and second, divide the twenty-three characters into two columns: one for "Criterion A"; one for "Criterion B."

C. If Part B is successfully accomplished, you will notice something obvious, unmistakable, and conspicuous about your two lists, and also about two specific characters we'll refer to as "Mr. X" and "Mr. Y." What is it that you notice about the list, and second, who are Mr. X and Mr. Y?

D. The final part of the question is this: From your results thus far, what can we deduce about Mr. X and Mr. Y?

IX

EPILOGUE:
THE LOST BOY

"Find the Stephen King"

Quiz 96

Stephen King has been mentioned in his own works six times. Match the "Stephen King" quotation in the left column with the work from which it was taken. (King's father's name, Donald King, was also used by King in his writing. That quotation is also included in this quiz.)

____1. "My own name, of course, is Steve King, and you'll pardon my intrusion on your mind—or I hope you will."

____2. "Those in favor of the former had James Herriott. Those in favor of the latter had Stephen King and *Inside View*. The difference, Dees thought, was that King made *his* stuff up."

____3. "You were starting to sound like a Stephen King novel for a while there, but it's not like that."

____4. Mr. Edwin King, who had Carrie for grade seven English, says: 'I don't know why I saved it.' "

____5. "She had asked the young man, Mr. Donald King by name, what his business was with Abby Freemantle, and he had replied: 'My business, ma'am, is pleasure.' "

____6. "With them were Lathrop Rounds (his nickname, as obscure as the Floating Dog Hotel, was El Katook), David 'Stugley' Grenier, and Eddie King—a bearded man whose spectacles were almost as fat as his gut."

____7. "I have never heard an Ozzy Osbourne record

and have no desire to do so, nor to read a novel by Robert McCammon, Stephen King, or V. C. Andrews."

A. *Carrie*
B. "The Library Policeman"
C. *The Stand*
D. *It*
E. "The Night Flier"
F. "The Blue Air Compressor"
G. *Thinner*

THE
ANSWERS

Quiz 1

1. Edward Dorn; *The Stand: The Complete & Uncut Edition* ("The Circle Opens"). 2. William Carlos Williams, *Paterson*; *It* (Part 2: "June of 1958"). 3. Friedrich Nietzsche; *Misery* (Part I: "Annie"). 4. AC/DC; *Different Seasons*. 5. John Lennon and Paul McCartney, "Drive My Car"; *Christine* (the chapter "LeBay Passes"). 6. George Seferis; *'Salem's Lot* (Part II: "The Emperor of Ice Cream"). 7. The Ramones; *Pet Sematary* (Part II: "The Micmac Burying Ground"). 8. Jack Barry, *Twenty-One; The Long Walk* (Chapter 6). 9. George Stark, *Machine's Way; The Dark Half* ("Prologue"). 10. Stephen Crane; *Four Past Midnight*. 11. K. C. and the Sunshine Band, "I'm Your Boogie Man"; *Skeleton Crew*. 12. Some kid; *It* (Epilogue: "Bill Denbrough Beats the Devil [II]") 13. The Who, "Won't Get Fooled Again"; *The Tommyknockers* (Book III: "The Tommyknockers"). 14. Folk song; *Cujo*. 15. Unknown World War I Top Sergeant; *The Long Walk* (Chapter 11). 16. Eddie Cochran, "Come on Everybody"; *Danse Macabre*. 17. Henry Ellender, *The Wolf; Cycle of the Werewolf*. 18. Mrs. Jean Underwood; *Rage*. 19. Matthew Arnold, "Dover Beach"; *Roadwork* (Part II: "December"). 20. Edward Dorn; *The Stand: The Complete & Uncut Edition* ("The Circle Closes").

Quiz 2

1. *Cujo*. 2. "The Wedding Gig," *Skeleton Crew*. 3. "The Doctor's Case." 4. *The Stand: The Complete & Uncut Edition*. 5. "The Sun Dog," *Four Past Midnight*. 6. "The Body," *Different Seasons*. 7. *Roadwork*. 8. "Graveyard Shift," *Night Shift*. 9. *The Dark Half*. 10. "The Last Rung on the Ladder," *Night Shift*. 11. *The Dead Zone*. 12. "Cain Rose Up," *Skeleton Crew*. 13. "Secret Window, Secret Garden," *Four Past Midnight*. 14. "Paranoid: A Chant" (poem), *Skeleton Crew*. 15. "Rainy Season." 16. *It*. 17. "The Fifth Quarter." 18. "Rita Hayworth and Shawshank Redemption," *Different Seasons*. 19. "You Know They Got a Hell of a Band." 20. *The Long Walk*.

Bonus Questions
21. "Brooklyn August" (poem). 22. "The Blue Air Compressor." 23. "The Glass Floor." 24. "My Pretty Pony." 25. "Before the Play."

Quiz 3
1. Former Sergeant First Class Roland Gibbs. 2. A baggie of marijuana. 3. The Kid. 4. Bobbi Anderson. 5. "Prince." 6. Tommy, a spirit who communicated with her via a ouija board. 7. Gareth. 8. Hemingford Home. 9. He said it to Jim Morrison of The Doors, and Jim replied, "You don't want to believe everything you read, man." 10. Her father's old pistol exploded in her hand as she tried to shoot "a hippie." 11. Arthur Stimson. 12. The Hotshot Rhythm Rangers & All-Time Boogie Band. 13. Stu Redman's childhood dog. 14. Sparx. 15. Lieutenant Calley.

Quiz 4
1. Nick Hopewell. 2. Craig Toomy. 3. "The Arizona Jew." 4. Massachusetts. 5. The University of California. 6. AP29. 7. L'Envoi. 8. Beirut. 9. "Shooting Stars Only." 10. Billy Crystal.

Quiz 5
1. "Sowing Season." 2. John Shooter. 3. John Kintner. 4. Derry, Maine. 5. *The Organ-Grinder's Boy*. It was an instant best-seller. 6. St. Martin's Press. 7. Bump. 8. Ted Milner. 9. $800,000. 10. Herb Creekmore.

Quiz 6
1. Curry & Trembo's All-Star Circus and Travelling Carnival. 2. Ardelia Lortz. 3. A gray felt hat. 4. Angle Street. 5. Sam's House of Pizza. 6. Duncan. 7. Pell's. 8. Thomas Jefferson. 9. Robert R. McCammon's *Swan Song*. 10. The 1980 Kansas City Royals.

Quiz 7
1. A Polaroid Sun 660 instant camera. 2. Megan (Meg). 3. Clyde Tombaugh. 4. Polaroidsville. 5. The

Emporium Galorium. 6. The Mellow Tiger. 7. $400.00. 8. A gentleman farmer ate between twelve and thirty-five vagabond young men. 9. A string tie. (She had begun sending one a year on his third birthday.) 10. A Wordstar 70 PC on which he received a message that the Sun Dog was "very hungry" and "very angry."

Quiz 8

People 1. Sally Ratcliffe. 2. Sean. 3. Lester Pratt. 4. Danforth Keeton III. 5. Raider. 6. Henry Beaufort. 7. Barney, "after the Don Knotts character on the old 'Andy Griffith Show.'" 8. Dr. Ray Van Allen. 9. Frank Jewett. 10. The Mislaburskis.

Places 1. Our Lady of Serene Waters. 2. Western Maine Realty and Insurance. 3. Akron, Ohio. 4. Hemphill's Market on Route 117. 5. Milton Academy. 6. The intersection of Willow and Ford streets. 7. In the Castle Building. 8. He said the coke came from the Plains of Leng, which are also mentioned in *The Eyes of the Dragon*. 9. Boston. 10. Junction City, Iowa.

Things 1. October 9th. 2. A 1956, signed Sandy Koufax baseball card (which was actually a Los Angeles Dodgers Sammy Koberg—lifetime record one win, three losses—baseball card.) 3. A Percodan—"or perhaps more than one." 4. He made shadow animals on the walls with his hands. 5. He had Brian throw mud on the clean sheets hanging on Wilma Jerzyck's clothesline. 6. A Bazun. 7. 1. "Always get the last word." 2. "Always make the first move when things get hot." 8. An *azka*. 9. Winning Ticket. 10. Re-heating coffee, making popcorn, and "putting a buzz under" cooled-off take-out.

Quiz 9

People 1. The Turtle. 2. Elmer. 3. Mr. Bissette. 4. Joanne Franks. 5. Mr. Harley. 6. Ms. Avery. 7. Beryl Evans. 8. Calvin Tower. 9. A young Eddie Dean playing basketball at the Portal of the Bear. 10. Aunt

Talitha Unwin. 11. David Quick. 12. Gasher. 13. Ardis. 14. Deidre the Mad. 15. Andrew Quick.

Places 1. The Great West Woods. 2. North Central Positronics, Ltd. 3. Dragon's Grave. 4. The Dark Tower. 5. The Mansion. 6. On the corner of Second and Forty-sixth in New York City. 7. The Manhattan Restaurant of the Mind. 8. It transformed into a living plaster monster ("the plaster-man") and then collapsed upon itself. 9. Northeast. 10. Lud to Candleton to Rilea to the Falls of the Hounds to Dasherville to Topeka.

Things 1. With their eye, mind, and heart. 2. "The world beneath the world." 3 #AA 24123 CX 755431297 L 14 4. The Creation of the Twelve Guardians. 5. A key and a rose. 6. "The place where many lives are joined by fate." 7. The Beams. 8. 1,B; 2,A; 3,C. 9. A key and a rose. 10. "The answer is a river." 11. 160 wheels. (Or 140 miles. Based on what Blaine told Roland and company, a wheel was equal to .875 miles.) 12. Strong apple beer. It was served to Roland and company by Aunt Talitha in River Crossing. 13. Z.Z. Top. 14. Oy. 15. "Hope for the best and expect the worst." 16. Death. 17. The Hanging Fountain of Lud. 18. "Bountiful." 19. A shadow. This was the "riddle-on-command" Eddie and Susannah asked Blaine the mono. 20. That the showdown always came.

Bonus Question 21. 97-89-83-79-73-71-67-61-59-53-47-43-41-37-31-29-23-19-17-13-11-7-5-3-2-1 (It was the prime numbers between 1 and 100 entered backwards.)

Quiz 10

1. Violet Mitla. 3. He was "one of New York's lesser-known certified public accountants." 3. Dennis Feeny. 4. Alex Trebeck. 5. American Grain. 6. In an apartment on the fourth floor of a nine-story building on Hawking Street in New York City. 7. He recited prime numbers in his head. 8. "Who were the Merry

202

Pranksters?" 9. "Scratch, scratch, scritchy-scratch." 10. "Because they can."

Quiz 11
1. In an upper-middle-class suburb of Portland, Oregon, that was known as Software City. 2. He worked for a computer company—"one of the giants." 3. "A motel with bathrobes on the bed and a hair-dryer in the bathroom." 4. Steve Earle and the Dukes. 5. A Mercedes diesel. 6. The Princess. 7. Lou Reed. 8. Intercourse. He wanted the postmark. 9. As the "Cookin'est Little Town in the Pacific Northwest." 10. The Cutting Edge. 11. The Tuneful Druggist. 12. White Rabbit. 13. The Rock-a-Boogie Restaurant. 14. Janis Joplin. 15. A Hound Dog. 16. A Chubby Checker. 17. A Big Bopper. 18. Rick Nelson. 19. Buddy Holly. 20. Rock and Roll Lullabye. 21. The Lizard King himself, Jim Morrison. 22. Otis Redding. 23. Elvis Presley. 24. "The Magic Bus." 25. Rock and roll.

Quiz 12
"Now he goes along the darksome road,
thither whence they say no one returns."
> —Catullus (You didn't really think I'd leave the quotation untranslated and send you back to your high school Latin texts, now did you?)

1. Michael McDowell, who also wrote the "Lover's Vow" segment of the film. 2. Mike. 3. Mitch. 4. *Tales from the Darkside.* 5. Twelve minutes a pound at 350°. 6. At least an hour. 7. "Lot 249." 8. "Cat From Hell." 9. "Lover's Vow." 10. He threw marbles on the floor, which caused her to slip and fall on the meat skewers. Timmy then pushed her into the roasting pan intended for him and slid her into the oven.

Quiz 13
1. J. 2. I. 3. G. 4. E. 5. D. 6. A. 7. C. 8. H. 9. B. 10. F.

Quiz 14

1. Drogan. 2. $100,000: $50,000 up front, and $50,000 on proof the cat was dead. 3. "One step up from street junk." 4. Midnight. 5. Milford. 6. Grape-Nuts. 7. You made mistakes. 8. $100. 9. He leaped onto his crotch and clawed him. (Ouch.) 10. It crawled its way down Halston's throat and into his stomach. When Drogan returned to the house, the cat crawled its way back out of Halston's mouth. (In the short story, the cat clawed and chewed its way out of Halston's stomach.)

Quiz 15

1. H. 2. M. 3. A. 4. D. 5. N. 6. G. 7. J. 8. C. 9. F. 10. I. 11. L. 12. O. 13. B. 14. E. 15. K.

Quiz 16

1. Daisy May. 2. The name of the mill was Bachman Textile Mills, and within the contest (and confines) of the film's script, it was named for the founder of the mills. But screenwriter John Esposito *really* named the mill as an homage to the "Richard Bachman" pseudonym used by Stephen King. 3. Jason Reed. 4. Warwick. 5. $200. 6. Greyhound. 7. Munson Textile. 8. The picker. 9. Minimum wage. 10. 11–7: the graveyard shift. 11. Diet Pepsi. 12. Tucker Cleveland. 13. Marshall Extermination. 14. "Burning baby flashback fuckup[s]." 15. "Hot meal[s]": raw American. 16. Wednesday. 17. Stevenson. 18. Porker. 19. Wheeling, West Virginia. 20. Castle Rock. 21. Charlie Carmichael. 22. She trashed his Cadillac with an axe. 23. Double pay. 24. Miami. 25. A damning OSHA report. 26. Brogan. 27. Moxie. 28. A Zippo. 29. He was eaten by the giant rat-bat-monster-in-the-water thing beneath the mill. 30. Carmichael. 31. By throwing a wine bottle at it. 32. Warwick stabbed her. 33. He was eaten by the giant rat-bat-monster-in-the-water thing beneath the mill. 34. It got caught in the picker. 35. He threw a Diet Pepsi can at the starter switch. (See Question 11.)

Quiz 17

1. J. 2. F. 3. H. 4. A. 5. B. 6. G. 7. I. 8. D. 9. E. 10. C.

Quiz 18

1. ". . . without it, what else was there?" 2. "Shot-gun," by Junior Walker & The Allstars. 3. 722. 4. Over a million. 5. Annie Wilkes. 6. Buster. 7. Eight. 8. Dom Perignon. 9. A 1965 Mustang. 10. The profanity. 11. His wife, Virginia. 12. Marcia Sindell. 13. The Sistine Chapel. (This was a question Annie asked Paul as she was reading *Misery's Child*. She said the only two divine things in the world were the Sistine Chapel and *Misery's Child*.) 14. 1871. 15. Twenty-four. 16. Kevin. (Kevin was the audience's selection on a "Love Connection" that Annie watched.) 17. A Royal. 18. An "N." 19. Eaton Corrasable Bond. 20. "Smudge." 21. A bent bobby pin. 22. *Memory Lane*. 23. *Misery's Challenge* and *Misery's Quest*. 24. 0012 0020509 42051. 25. "Family Feud." 26. He typed the word "fuck" without spaces seven times (visibly) in lower case. 27. Liberace. 28. Denise. 29. She used only fresh tomatoes, never canned, and added a little Spam. 30. A large carving knife. 31. She noticed that her ceramic penguin had been moved. (It always faced due south.) 32. A sledge-hammer. 33. Left foot, right foot. 34. "There is a justice higher than that of man. I will be judged by Him." 35. In the cellar. 36. He knocked over a barbecue grill. 37. Annie killed him with a shotgun. 38. By slamming her in the face with a heavy pig figurine. 39. *The Higher Education of J. Philip Stone*. 40. In a restaurant, dressed as a waitress pushing a dessert cart.

Quiz 19

1. F. 2. L. 3. W. 4. E. 5. P. 6. U. 7. Q. 8. A. 9. C. 10. N. 11. M. 12. K. 13. V. 14. O. 15. Y. 16. G. 17. B. 18. T. 19. S. 20. D. 21. X. 22. I. 23. J. 24. H. 25. R.

Quiz 20

1. The Paramount. (It was the Alladin in the book.) 2. In among the sheets hanging on the clothesline. 3.

Bill. 4. FALSE. He had a long ponytail. 5. Beverly By Hand. (It was Beverly Fashions in the book.) 6. Eddie wasn't married in the film. (In the book, his wife's name was Myra.) 7. He was a comedian. (In the book, he was a disc jockey.) 8. "Get Leno." (This was Richie's response to the question about Carson posed by his manager after Richie told him he was going to Maine.) 9. "Perfect Strangers." (In the book, it was "Family Feud.") 10. Richie's mother's "solid silver" earrings. (In the book, they melted down Ben's silver dollars.)

Quiz 21

11. Bill Denbrough. 12. Mike Hanlon. (In the book, Bill bought Silver himself when he returned to Derry.) 13. "Rest in Peace/Richie Tozier/Born 1950–Died 1990." 14. Two Aces of Spades. (In the book, the Aces were red and blue.) 15. Greco. 16. The Chop Suey Chinese Restaurant. (In the book, it was the Jade of the Orient, and it was a reunion *lunch*.) 17. 1960. (In the book, it was 1930.) 18. "Sing 'Kumbaya'?" (Richie asked the question "What the hell you gonna do now?" after Bill, Ben, Bev, and Eddie grasped hands before their descent into the sewers. He then offered his own exquisitely sarcastic response, "Sing 'Kumbaya'?" This cracks me up.) 19. TRUE. (In the film, that is. In the book, he was part of the "Love and Desire" ritual, and thus had made love to at least one person, Bev.) 20. Richie carried it out of the sewers after It was defeated. (In the book, they left his body in the sewers.)

Quiz 22

1. B. 2. E. 3. A. 4. I. 5. G. 6. J. 7. C. 8. F. 9. D. 10. H.

Quiz 23

1. Sally. 2. Scott. 3. Chip Conway. 4. Kate. 5. The Liberty Blue Jays. 6. Twenty-seven years. 7. "Soupy Sales." 8. 12. 9. *The War of the Worlds*. 10. His wal-

let. 11. He flew off a trestle bridge on his bike while chased by the hoods that killed Jim's brother. 12. Richard Lawson. 13. An orange. 14. *The Dead Zone*. She played Sarah Bracknell. 15. They hung her from the rafters in a barn, making it look like suicide. 16. Kansas City. 17. Chief Pappas. 18. They showed him "the face": They let him see their rotted corpses as they actually were. 19. David North. 20. A blue and red cap with a "W" in a triangle on the front. 21. Officer Bob Nell. 22. *It*. (Although it seems as though he apparently changed his first name from "Aloysius" to "Bob" for this film!) 23. "Milford." It was a cemetery. 24. Carl Mueller. 25. Nothing. "You can't kill what's already dead." 26. They blew it up. 27. His foot and leg caught fire. 28. Lawson stabbed him. 29. He went to "a better place" where his mom and dad were waiting for him. 30. He gave him a dime and two pennies: 12¢. They were "good luck coins" his big brother had once given him.

Quiz 24

1. Y. 2. O. 3. G. 4. B. 5. R. 6. K. 7. A. 8. DD. 9. U. 10. S. 11. Q. 12. J. 13. F. 14. CC. 15. W. 16. T. 17. L. 18. C. 19. E. 20. P. 21. H. 22. V. 23. M. 24. AA. 25. I. 26. Z. 27. D 28. X 29. BB 30. N

Quiz 25

1-1. David Bowie's song "Golden Years." 1-2. Rick. 1-3. Seventy. 1-4. His birthday was November 28th, and he would be seventy-one. 1-5. A key card and thumbprint. 1-6. Falco Plains Agricultural Testing facility. 1-7. Red. 1-8. $2 billion. 1-9. 10884. 1-10. Secondary Override Delta. 1-11. Dr. Tommy Jackson. 1-12. Mail-order taxidermy. "People pay good money for well-mounted specimens." 1-13. Apple Macintosh. 1-14. To tell him he had failed his eye exam. 1-15. Terry Spann. 1-16. General Louis Crewes. 1-17. Gina. 1-18. Regeneration. Attempting to accelerate the healing process in living tissue. 1-19. It was called KR-3. According to Todhunter, it was "a byproduct of a harmless chemical reaction." 1-20. It disappeared. 1-21. Jude Andrews. 1-22. Dr. Ackerman. 1-23. Ethan. 1-24. Harlan had less "floaters"; fewer spots in his eyes. 1-25. Andrews killed him and dumped his car off a ferry landing into a river. 1-26. The first Monday of each month. 1-27. In the toilet tank in his hotel room. 1-28. A Zippo. 1-29. His hair began turning brown again. 1-30. We can't know for sure, but he might have attended Ewen High with Carrie White. We find out in the credits that Billy's last name was DeLois, and since there was a Billy DeLois who went to Ewen High (he cut French I) in 1979 with Carrie, and since he'd be 29 or 30 now, and since the Billy in "Golden Years" looks about that age, it's a fair guess that they're the same guy. (If so, then this fact was obviously planted as an "inside joke" by King.) (Also, Phil Lenkowsky, who played Billy DeLois, played Maddox in the "Lover's Vow" segment [written by Michael McDowell] of *Tales from the Darkside: The Movie*, the film that also contained the film version of Stephen King's short story "Cat From Hell." See the *Tales from the Darkside* and "Cat From Hell" quizzes in this volume.)

Quiz 26

2-1. A Zippo. 2-2. Fourteen percent in less than a month. 2-3. His father. 2-4. Bacon and eggs. 2-5. "Perfect paranoia is perfect awareness." 2-6. He told him he would perform some dental surgery with a power drill and a Number 2 drill bit. Sometimes he performed the surgery with the mouth open; sometimes through the cheek. He didn't use Novocaine, and there was usually a great deal of blood. 2-7. Vitamin C. 2-8. "He wanted to see time fly." (This was a joke Billy told Harlan.) 2-9. According to Terry, "Fruits" were the members of the United States House of Representatives, and "Nuts" were the members of the United States Senate. 2-10. Suzi's Unisex Express. 2-11. Rita. 2-12. Jude Andrews. 2-13. In the front hall closet. 2-14. Maui, Idaho, and Vermont. 2-

15. That she couldn't keep up with Harlan anymore; she was too old.

Quiz 27
3-1. Inside a stuffed teddy bear. 3-2. "Baseball." 3-3. "Over 9 innings, 5 runs on 12 hits, 6 errors, 4 men left on base, and visiting team, 8 runs on 13 hits, 12 errors, 5 men left on base, and the winning pitcher, number 12." (It decoded to a phone number.) 3-4. Steven Dent. 3-5. *The Falco Plains Free Democrat.* 3-6. 1:45 A. M. 3-7. Three years. 3-8. Doc Pulaski. 3-9. They put it in the meat locker at Warren's Market. 3-10. Jude Andrews. 3-11. In a light bulb in a lamp in the living room. The receiving unit was in the basement. 3-12. She wrote "Just like old times" in lipstick on a mirror in the front hall and signed it with a "T" in a heart. 3-13. Chicago. 3-14. Whitney. 3-15. The North Gate Mall parking lot.

Quiz 28
4-1. Red. 4-2. Gina's cousin Cecil. 4-3. King Ramses. He was 2,000 years old. 4-4. His car exploded thanks to a bomb wired to the ignition by Jude Andrews. 4-5. He threw it away. 4-6. John Rainbird. (He was in *Firestarter.*) 4-7. Jude Andrews. 4-8. On his father's grave. 4-9. He had orders that said that Crewes was restricted to base. 4-10. Having Harlan and Gina shoplift and get arrested. They would then be locked up by *civil* authorities and kept safe. 4-11. "Lee Harvey Oswald." (Being shot while in custody.) 4-12. They ran into the electrified fence at the testing facility after they got out of Todhunter's van. 4-13. Make bookends. 4-14. "Magic." 4-15. In his shoe.

Quiz 29
5-1. "Castigate." 5-2. Waste them. 5-3. Arnie and Bill: left front, scatterguns; Vinnie and Craig: right front, same; Jack and Sean: rear tires, service revolvers. 5-4. Three scarecrows with signs on them that said, "Moe," "Larry," and "Curly." 5-5. Stephen

King. 5-6. "Drive the bus and put your mouth in neutral." 5-7. Mrs. Rogers. 5-8. A truck driver for the Chemical Cartage Company, Inc. 5-9. A-16 A-18 Database. 5-10. Burton. 5-11. "Sparrowhawk." 5-12. It was his square-dancing night. 5-13. In the trunk of Major Moreland's car. 5-14. The electronic equipment in the truck went crazy, the sun came up at midnight, there was an earthquake, and Harlan glowed with a green light. 5-15. "This guy's full 'o green light!"

Quiz 30

6-1. God. 6-2. People leaving their Christmas lights up all year long, and plastic Christmas trees. 6-3. Head mounting. 6-4. St. Louis. 6-5. Pasadena. 6-6. 744. 6-7. Apartment 3. 6-8. Level 4. 6-9. Steak and eggs, sunnyside up. 6-10. His eyes glowed green and he caused another earthquake. 6-11. Francie. 6-12. "Pigs." 6-13. He kneed him in the balls. 6-14. Jude Andrews killed her. 6-15. E1K602.

Quiz 31

7-1. Sybil. 7-2. Richard Rogers. 7-3. 4027. 7-4. When Todhunter zapped it with his "rays," it began running backwards and then it disappeared. 7-5. Purple. 7-6. Two weeks' salary and her sugar ration. 7-7. Because she never stopped thinking. 7-8. Automatic weapons. (Some of them looked like AK-47s?) 7-9. "[T]wist [off] something else that's attached to [your] body." (Andrews had already twisted Burton's ear.) 7-10. That nothing ever really ended. 7-11. Andrews shot him. 7-12. Police sharpshooters shot them on Jude Andrews's command. 7-13. Jude Andrews shot him. 7-14. Burton stabbed him with a hypodermic filled with a sedative after Harlan refused to leave Gina and go with Terry and General Crewes. 7-15. "Harlan?"

(A DRAWING OF) THREE BONUS QUESTIONS

7-16. He was "the first man in the history of the world ever to have travelled backward in time." 7-17. "No more." 7-18. "Wish upon wish upon day/I believe, O Lord/I believe all the way."

Quiz 32
1-L-i. 2-Q-m. 3-I-o. 4-C-h. 5-D-b. 6-T-d. 7-A-s. 8-O-f. 9-K-n. 10-G-k. 11-E-c. 12-N-t. 13-R-a. 14-P-r. 15-F-g. 16-M-p. 17-B-e. 18-S-l. 19-J-q. 20-H-j.

Quiz 33
1. C. *Stephen King's "It"* 2. J. *'Salem's Lot* 3. V. *Silver Bullet* 4. B. *Christine* 5. D. *Cujo*; U. *Cat's Eye* 6. A. *The Dead Zone* 7. S. *The Woman in the Room* 8. N. *Creepshow 2* 9. K. *Carrie* 10. G. *Pet Sematary* 11. L. *Creepshow* 12. F. *The Shining* 13. P. *Children of the Corn* 14. Q. *The Last Rung on the Ladder* 15. M. *Stand By Me*; O. *Misery*; 16. I. *Maximum Overdrive* 17. T. *Stephen King's "Graveyard Shift"* 18. E. *Tales from the Darkside: The Movie* 19. H. *The Lawnmower Man* 20. R. *The Running Man*

Quiz 34
1-J-j; 2-G-d; 3-I-a; 4-F-b; 5-E-e; 6-A-f; 7-C-i; 8-D-h; 9-B-g; 10-H-c.

Quiz 35
1. F. 2. T. 3. E. 4. G. 5. R. 6. S. 7. I. 8. H. 9. Q. 10. C. 11. D. 12. J. 13. L. 14. P. 15. O. 16. K. 17. B. (Translation: "Davey Hartwell was a man who walked like he owned half of the world and had him a deadlock on the rest.") 18. M. 19. N. 20. A.

Bonus Question
21. Gasher, to Jake Chambers (*The Dark Tower III: The Waste Lands*)

Quiz 36
1. B, F. 2. D, G. 3. G, H. 4. M, O. 5. A, L. 6. E, H, I, N. 7. C, F. 8. F, J. 9. C, L, M. 10. B, F, K.

Quiz 37

A, 5; *The Dark Half*. B, 2; "My Pretty Pony." C, 3; *The Stand* and *The Stand: The Complete & Uncut Edition*. D, 14; *It*. E, 12; *Cujo*. F, 1; *The Stand* and *The Stand: The Complete & Uncut Edition*. G, 13; *Firestarter*. H, 11; *The Talisman*. I, 10; "The End of the Whole Mess." J, 4; *The Dark Half*. K, 15; *Christine*. L, 7; *The Shining*. M, 8; *Misery*. N, 9; *The Dark Half*. O, 6.

Quiz 38

1. TRUE. (*Carrie*) 2. FALSE. It was in New Hampshire. (*The Talisman*) 3. FALSE. It was in October of 1929. (*It*) 4. FALSE. He did include works by Erle Stanley Gardner and Louis L'Amour, as well as Perry Mason novels and Jake Logan westerns, but no Stephen King. ("Rita Hayworth and Shawshank Redemption" from *Different Seasons*) 5. TRUE. (*The Plant*) 6. TRUE. ("The Mangler" from *Night Shift*) 7. FALSE. It was $514 an ounce. ("Word Processor of the Gods" from *Skeleton Crew*) 8. TRUE. (*People, Places, and Things*) 9. FALSE. It was "Not a very nice guy." (*The Dark Half*) 10. TRUE. The *title* "Eye of the Crow" *was* written by Mort Rainey, but the answer is also FALSE, because Mort stole John Kintner's short story "Crowfoot Mile," renamed it "Eye of the Crow," and submitted it as his own work. ("Secret Window, Secret Garden" from *Four Past Midnight*) 11. TRUE. (And even though I *am* the author of *The Woody Allen Companion*, this is not just an unconscionable plug. *Purple Rose* is mentioned in *The Dark Tower II: The Drawing of the Three*, and I couldn't resist.) 12. FALSE. Uncle Al *did* show up every July, but it was for a salmon and fresh peas dinner. (*Cycle of the Werewolf*) 13. TRUE. ("For the Birds") 14. TRUE. ("The Sun Dog" from *Four Past Midnight*) 15. FALSE. It was Pig Pen. ("Cain Rose Up" from *Skeleton Crew*) 16. TRUE. (*The Shining*) 17. FALSE. It was Bill Hinch, the Lord High Executioner. (*The Eyes of the Dragon*) 18. TRUE. (*Pet Sematary*) 19.

FALSE. He grabbed her "oh-so-grabbable-tit." (*Thinner*) 20. FALSE. She was a 1958 red Plymouth Fury. (*Christine*) 21. TRUE. (*The Stand: The Complete & Uncut Edition*) 22. TRUE. ("The Reach" from *Skeleton Crew*) 23. FALSE. It was lime Jell-O. 24. TRUE. ("The Gunslinger and the Dark Man" from *The Dark Tower: The Gunslinger*) 25. BET ON IT. (From the *It* dedication)

Quiz 39

1. "The Dreaded X" (in *Gauntlet 2*, 1991) 2. *Four Past Midnight* 3. "For Owen" (from *Skeleton Crew*) 4. *The Dark Tower III: The Waste Lands* 5. "The Lonesome Death of Jordy Verrill" (from *Creepshow*) 6. *Rage* 7. "Paranoid: A Chant" (from *Skeleton Crew*) 8. "Trucks" (from *Night Shift*) 9. *Cycle of the Werewolf* 10. *Needful Things* 11. "On Becoming a Brand Name" (in *Fear Itself: The Horror Fiction of Stephen King*) 12. "The Raft" (from *Skeleton Crew*) 13. *Misery* 14. *Pet Sematary* 15. "The Mist" (from *Skeleton Crew*) 16. "Quitters, Inc." from *Night Shift*) 17. "The Langoliers" (from *Four Past Midnight*) 18. *Creepshow* 19. *Slade* 20. *Cujo* 21. "You Gotta Put on the Gruesome Mask and Go Booga-Booga" (from *TV Guide*, December 5, 1981)

Quiz 40

1. I. 2. O. 3. G. 4. A. 5. N. 6. D. 7. L. 8. B. 9. V. 10. Q. 11. J. 12. T. 13. C. 14. E. 15. F. 16. EE. 17. AA. 18. II. 19. P. 20. K. 21. U. 22. GG. 23. HH. 24. FF. 25. M. 26. R. 27. X. 28. S. 29. H. 30. DD. 31. CC. 32. W. 33. BB. 34. Z. 35. Y.

Quiz 41

1. *S*hining 2. *T*ommyknocker 3. *E*yes of the Dragon 4. *P*et Sematary 5. *H*ell 6. *E*nd 7. *N*ight Surf 8. *E*dwin 9. *D*rawing of the Three 10. *W*alk 11. *I*t 12. *N*ight Flier 13. *K*now what you need 14. *I* am the doorway 15. *N*ona 16. *G*unslinger

The first letters of the answers spell out STEPHEN
EDWIN KING.

Quiz 42
1. B. 2. F. 3. AA. 4. A. 5. K. 6. D. 7. G. 8. E. 9.
C. 10. L. 11. H. 12. Z. 13. I. 14. M. 15. BB. 16. N.
17. J. 18. V. 19. X. 20. Y. 21. W. 22. O. 23. CC. 24.
P. 25. S. 26. U. 27. DD. 28. T. 29. R. 30. Q.

Quiz 43
1. *Carrie:* He burned to death in the school gym-
   nasium after being knocked unconscious by the
   falling "pig's blood" milk bucket.
2. *'Salem's Lot:* They were both crucified upside
   down.
3. *Rage:* They slit their noses.
4. *The Shining:* They resorted to cannibalism.
5. *Night Shift:* 5a. ". . . some huge rats . . ." 5b.
   He was eaten by the Magna Mater rat in the
   mill's sub-sub-basement. 5c. A Zippo. 5d.
   When he saw eyes peering at him through slits
   in his fingers, he drenched his hands with kero-
   sene and set them afire to get rid of the aliens
   infesting his hands. (It didn't work.) 5e. An
   arm. 5f. In the closet. 5g. A dead cat covered
   with maggots. 5h. He was killed by a miniature
   nuclear explosion set off by living, toy soldiers.
   5i. They threw Molotov cocktails into it. 5j.
   From a dead cat. 5k. Her head. 5l. Forty years.
   5m. A half-quart of cherry Kool-Aid. 5n. An
   operative would be sent to break both of Alvin's arms. 5o. Voodoo. 5p. Cornhusks. 5q. She
   committed suicide by jumping from the top
   floor of an insurance building in Los Angeles.
   5r. "A hammer." 5s. It is assumed he was
   turned into a vampire when he got drunk, went
   into the Lot at night, and was never seen again.
   5t. Marilyn Monroe.
6. *The Stand: The Complete & Uncut Edition*: He
   died of appendicitis during emergency surgery

performed by Stu Redman. Stu was operating while following along in a medical book.

7. *The Long Walk: Massa's on De Cold, Cold Road* or *The Tell-Tale Stride*.

8. *The Dead Zone:* "I confess." (It was written in lipstick on a sign hanging around his [quite dead] neck.)

9. *Firestarter:* They pulled out her fingernails.

10. *Roadwork:* Forty.

11. *Cujo:* Frank Dodd.

12. *Creepshow:* 12a. He used it as the centerpiece of his "back-from-the-dead" Father's Day cake. 12b. He got turned into a human weed and then blew his head off with a shotgun. 12c. Henry fed her to the thing in the crate. 12d. Three: Becky Vickers, Richard Wentworth, and Richard Vickers. 12e. Inside Upson Pratt.

13. *The Running Man:* False; he was on "The Running Man" only.

14. *The Dark Tower: The Gunslinger:* 14a. Sylvia Pittston. 14b. Gallows Hill on Farson Road. 14c. A living skull covered with slime. 14d. Lazarus. 14e. The Hanged Man.

15. *Different Seasons:* 15a. He castrated a classmate with a piece of rusty metal. 15b. To get rid of the smell of the cat he had roasted in his oven. 15c. He was killed in a jeep accident during basic training at Fort Benning, Georgia. 15d. The severed head of Sandra Stansfield said, "Thank you, Dr. McCarron."

16. *Christine:* A piece of hamburger. Barry Gottfried saved her life by administering the Heimlich Maneuver on her.

17. *Pet Sematary*: She was "kilt on the highway."

18. *The Talisman*: "Your mother died screaming."

19. *Thinner:* "Never."

20. *Cycle of the Werewolf:* Brady Kincaid.

21. *Skeleton Crew:* 21a. Aggie Bibber. 21b. Kenny Griffen. 21c. He was electrocuted when the monkey knocked a Philco radio into the bathtub

while he was bathing. 21d. From cancer or maybe renal failure. 21e. He shot himself. 21f. The first and second fingers of his left hand. 21g. "Ten." 21h. He "drowned it in the sink and wrote it up/in folder GAMMA." 21i. He learned how to make them race in a matchbox. 21j. He "made a pipe bomb out of the celluloid . . . off the backs of a deck of playing cards." 21k. He got into Brower's car in Bombay, accidentally started it, and crashed into a stone wall. 21l. A giant sand hand. 21m. The smell of age, a smell "common only to museums and mausoleums." 21n. Rats. 21o. "Dying." 21p. His earlobes. 21q. He was crushed to death under "Uncle Otto's truck." 21r. A tarantula. 21s. Kill her and mail her body to General Delivery, Lima, Indiana; North Pole, New Hampshire; Intercourse, Pennsylvania; or Kunkle, Iowa. 21t. By saying, "Gyaagin! Gyaagin! Hastur degryon Yos-soth-oth!" 21u. She committed suicide. 21v. He lost it to frostbite in 1938 when his Bombardier Skiddoo broke through the frozen Reach and Stewie ended up in the frigid water.

22. *It:* Blood, flesh, and hair.

23. *The Dark Tower II: The Drawing of the Three:* Under a chickenhouse in Sedonville, Connecticut.

24. *The Eyes of the Dragon:* Human skin.

25. *Misery:* Charlotte Evelyn-Hyde's hand protruding from the earth after she'd been declared dead and then buried.

26. *The Tommyknockers:* A flying Coke machine.

27. *The Dark Half:* Alexis Machine stabbed him in the left eye with a small steel rod.

28. *Four Past Midnight:* 28a. Her body was pulled outside a plane through a crack in the hull. 28b. He was nailed to the top of a garage cabinet with a screwdriver. 28c. She used a funnel-shaped proboscis, and the fear looked like bloody snot. 28d. He cut her throat and drained her blood into a basin.

29. *The Dark Tower III: The Waste Lands:* The doctors called it mandrus, but everyone else called it whore's blossoms.
30. *Needful Things:* Nettie Cobb buried a cleaver in her skull.

Bonus: "One More Morbid Moment"
"Sneakers": A hacksaw was used, and his hand was left floating in a toilet bowl.

Quiz 44
"JACK TORRANCE" (*The Shining*) 44a. Becky. 44b. Zeiss-lkon. 44c. *My Life in the Twentieth Century.* 44d. Phyllis Sandler. 44e. He was killed in a boiler explosion at the Overlook Hotel.

Quiz 45
"CARRIE WHITE" (*Carrie*) 45a. September 21, 1963. 45b. Woolworth's. 45c. 94.3°. (Normal is 98.6°.) 45d. 190/100. (Normal is 120/80.) 45e. First, she set off the sprinklers, which resulted in multiple electrocutions. She then caused several explosions in Chamberlain, resulting in a huge, devastating fire.

Quiz 46
"TAD TRENTON" (*Cujo*) 46a. A Mighty Marvel calendar. 46b. Fig bars, olives, and Slim Jims. 46c. Frank Dodd, the Castle Rock Strangler. 46d. Greedo. 46e. "A Frisbee."

Quiz 47
"BILLY HALLECK" (*Thinner*) 47a. "The Incredible Shrinking Man." 47b. "[A] steaming mound of scrambled eggs, an English muffin with raisins, [and] five strips of crisp country-style bacon." 47c. Miller. 47d. (203) 555-9231. 47e. He had X-rays, a CAT-scan, an EEG, and an EKG.

Quiz 48
"MOTHER ABAGAIL" (*The Stand* and *The Stand: The Complete & Uncut Edition*) 48a. John Freemantle.

48b. 1982. It was a gift from her kin, Cathy and David. 48c. "The Old Rugged Cross"; "How I Love My Jesus"; "Camp Meeting in Georgia"; "When Johnny Comes Marching Home"; "Marching Through Georgia"; "Goober Peas"; and "Tenting Tonight on the Old Campground." 48d. Pride. 48e. In *The Stand*, 1977; in *The Stand: The Complete & Uncut Edition*, 1982.

Quiz 49

"RAY GARRATY" (*The Long Walk*) 49a. His name was Jim Garraty, and he was taken away by the Squads and never seen again. 49b. Mrs. Elwell brought them ice-cold water and Ray got water cramps. 49c. He sat down, took his three warnings as he worked out the cramp, and then got up. 49d. "The Crowd." 49e. RD 1, Pownal, Maine, in Androscoggin County.

Quiz 50

"BILL DENBROUGH" (*It*) 50a. Audra Philpott. (Her stage name was Audra Phillips.) 50b. "Why does a story have to be socio-anything? Politics . . . culture . . . history . . . aren't those natural ingredients in any story, if it's told well? I mean . . . can't you . . . just let a story be a story?" (Any paraphrased rendering of the substance of that quotation scores. It shows you're paying attention!) 50c. Gulf parrafin. 50d. "He thrusts his fists against the posts and still insists he sees the ghost." 50e. Richard Thomas.

Quiz 51

"ANNIE WILKES" (*Misery*) 51a. In the linen closet. 51b. $506.17. 51c. A Jeep Cherokee. 51d. Her "Laughing Place" in the hills. She had taken the name from the Uncle Remus stories, specifically the one in which Brer Rabbit tells Brer Fox about his "Laughing Place." 51e. September 9, 1982.

Quiz 52

"ROLAND LeBAY" (*Christine*) 52a. George. 52b. Veronica. 52c. September 1957. 52d. $2,100. (The original asking price was $3,000.) 52e. 71.

Quiz 53

"DAVID DRAYTON" ("The Mist") 53a. He was a commercial artist. 53b. Dick Muehler. 53c. The Flat Earth Society. 53d. The University of Maine. 53e. "Beans and False Perspective."

Quiz 54

"SUNLIGHT GARDENER" (*The Talisman*) 54a. Robert Gardener. 54b. Osmond. 54c. "I'll Be a Sunbeam for Jesus." 54d. Psalm 37. He changed the words. 54e. *The Sunlight of Jesus*.

Quiz 55

"ARDELIA LORTZ" ("The Library Policeman") 55a. One gold earring. 55b. *The Speaker's Companion*. 55c. *Swan Song*. 55d. $2.00. 55e. 1960.

Quiz 56

"POLLY CHALMERS" (*Needful Things*) 56a. Duke Sheehan's. 56b. A dark polyester pants suit, a white silk blouse, L'Eggs Nearly Nude pantyhose, and low heels. 56c. Lorraine. 56d. Kelton Chalmers. 56e. You Sew and Sew.

Quiz 57

"JIM GARDENER" (*The Tommyknockers*) 57a. "If it's gratis, grab it." 57b. "Leighton Street." 57c. Sunday River. 57d. *The Radiation Cycle*. 57e. Type "O."

Quiz 58

"NICK HOPEWELL" ("The Langoliers") 58a. Thirty-five. 58b. Track down his father and tell him that Nick had tried his best "to atone for the day behind the church in Belfast." 58c. "Special Operations." 58d. Mr. O'Banion 58e. His knee.

Quiz 59

"KURT DUSSANDER/ARTHUR DENKER" ("Apt Pupil" from *Different Seasons*) 59a. The Cleveland Torso Murderer, The Zodiac, Mr. X., and Springheel Jack. 59b. Glade. 59c. West Berlin. 59d. "The Blood-Fiend of Patin." 59e. Ancient Age.

Quiz 60

"FLAGG" (*The Eyes of the Dragon*) 60a. He was the Lord High Executioner. (Figures, right?) 60b. Becoming "dim." 60c. Obsidian. 60d. A kleffa carrot. 60e. The Shaking Disease.

Quiz 61

"IT/PENNYWISE/BOB GRAY" (*It*) 61a. It's awakening and feeding cycle consisted of fourteen to twenty months every twenty-seven years. 61b. The Kitchener Ironworks explosion. 61c. Prostate cancer, a brain tumor, and turning his tongue to mush. 61d. May 31, 1985. 61e. "Son, you did real good."

Quiz 62

"CHARLIE McGEE" (*Firestarter*) 62a. March 24th. 62b. *Winnie the Pooh, Mr. Toad*, and *Willie Wonka's Great Glass Elevator*. 62C. Tashmore Pond. 62d. Orasin. 62e. Louis Tranter.

Quiz 63

"MARTY COSLAW" (*Cycle of the Werewolf*) 63a. Four. 63b. Kate. 63c. The left eye. 63d. "End it." 63e. Herman.

Quiz 64

"MORTON RAINEY" ("Secret Window, Secret Garden" from *Four Past Midnight*) 64a. *The Delacourt Family*. 64b. "The Couch of the Comatose Writer" and "The World-Famous Mort Rainey Sofa." 64e. 92 Kansas Street. 64d. $4,900. 64e. A Royal.

Quiz 65

"JUD CRANDALL" (*Pet Sematary*) 65a. Norma. 65b. H-102. 65c. Spot. 65d. 1914. 65e. Black Label.

Quiz 66

"KURT BARLOW" (*'Salem's Lot*) 66a. Romanian, Magyar, or Hungarian. 66b. He got in "disguised" as a Hepplewhite sideboard. 66c. Garlic and roses. 66d. The Dark Father, Satan. 66e. Bram Stoker.

Quiz 67

"THAD BEAUMONT" (*The Dark Half*) 67a. John Wesley Harding. 67b. Sixty. 67c. One of the FBI men who questioned Thad after Miriam Cowley's murder. 67d. Shayla Beaumont. 67e. Harry Black.

Quiz 68

"BEN RICHARDS" (*The Running Man*) 68a. $15.50. 68b. 165 pounds. 68c. 126. 68d. 2025. 68e. *God Is an Englishman, Not As a Stranger*, and *The Pleasure of Serving*.

Quiz 69

"FRANK DODD" (*The Dead Zone*) 69a. Henrietta. 69b. Alma Frechette. 69c. Carol Dunbarger. 69d. Tom Harrison. 69e. Wilkinson Sword razor blades.

Quiz 70

"CHARLIE DECKER" (*Rage*) 70a. Dicky Cable. 70b. They met at Jessie Decker Hannaford's wedding. (Jessie was burned to death a year after her wedding.) 70c. "The Bach Fugue for Storm Windows in A Minor." (Charlie's mother had been playing Bach when, at the age of four, Charlie broke all the storm windows in their house with rocks.) 70d. Play ragtime music. 70e. A Scripto.

Quiz 71

"LARD ASS HOGAN" ("The Revenge of Lard Ass Hogan" from "The Body" from *Different Seasons*)

71a. David Hogan. 71b. Mr. Bancichek. 71c. Three-quarters of a bottle of castor oil. 71d. In the March 1975 issue of *Esquire* magazine. 71e. Andy Lindberg.

Quiz 72
"REGINALD 'POP' MERRILL" ("The Sun Dog" from *Four Past Midnight*) 72a. The Mad-Hatters. 72b. $90.00 72c. Diamond Blue Tip. 72d. A 1959 Chevrolet. (It was maintained free of charge at Sonny's Texaco, the fallout of a loan Pop had once made to the proprietor, Sonny Jackett.) 72e. Approximately $19,000.

Quiz 73
"THE TICK-TOCK MAN" (*The Dark Tower III: The Waste Lands*) 73a. Dirty gray-blond. 73b. A small gold clock in a coffin-shaped glass box on a silver chain. 73c. He threw a knife into her chest. 73b. David Quick. 73e. Richard Fannin, the Wizard.

Quiz 74
1. A. 2. I. 3. D. 4. A. 5. K. 6. J. 7. E. 8. A. 9. K. 10. F. 11. B. 12. A. 13. H. 14. A. 15. G. 16. C.

Quiz 75
1, UU. 2, B. 3, C. 4, K. 5, D. 6, II. 7, T. 8, A. 9, N. 10, Q. 11, E. 12, Y. 13, J. 14, L. 15, P. 16, H. 17, O. 18, JJ. 19, R. 20, S. 21, DD. 22, W. 23, NN. 24, RR. 25, I. 26, LL. 27, V. 28, X. 29, FF. 30, HH. 31, PP. 32, WW. 33, GG. 34, G. 35, M. 36, XX. 37, VV. 38, KK. 39, F. 40, BB. 41, MM. 42, U. 43, CC. 44, Z. 45, EE. 46, OO. 47, SS. 48, QQ. 49, TT. 50, AA.

Quiz 76
1. YY. 2. GG. 3. B. 4. BBB. 5. A. 6. WW. 7. EE. 8. AAA. 9. S. 10. H. 11. TT. 12. N. 13. K. 14. UU. 15. D. 16. I. 17. CCC. 18. W. 19. Z. 20. T. 21. O. 22. F. 23. G. 24. VV. 25. OO. 26. XX. 27. MM. 28. ZZ. 29. NN. 30. JJ. 31. Y. 32. BB. 33. P. 34. M. 35. Q. 36. KK. 37. RR. 38. FF. 39. U. 40. SS. 41. L. 42.

QQ. 43. C. 44. CC. 45. J. 46. DD. 47. E. 48. HH.
49. II. 60. LL. 51. R. 52. V. 53. AA. 54. X. 55. PP.

Quiz 77
1. D. Harold; 2. E. Sandra; 3. X. Jimmy; 4. UU.
Steffy; 5. Y. Lily Cavanaugh; 6. B. Wilma; 7. II or
WW. Andy; 8. XX. Ruth; 9. AA. Stella; 10. Z. Co-
lette; 11. C. Lonnie; 12. A. George; 13. G. Richard;
14. H. Vera; 15. Q. Norman; 16. F. Michael; 17. O.
Monica; 18. R. Cassandra; 19. VV. Bart; 20. TT.
Lina; 21. W. Ophelia; 22. P. Mary; 23. V. Cora; 24.
M. Bill; 25. N. Mark; 26. I. Milt; 27. S. William; 28.
K. Harvey; 29. U. Reg; 30. L. Ralph; 31. J. Mort;
32. T. Thad; 33. GG. Donna; 34. FF. Sheila; 35. HH.
Billy; 36. CC. Louis; 37. SS. Rita; 38. DD. Lester;
39. EE. John; 40. LL. Sarah; 41. RR. Marjorie; 42.
QQ. Alice; 43. MM. Vicky; 44. PP. Rita; 45. BB.
Jim; 46. OO. Wendy; 47. KK. Francie; 48. II or WW.
Andy; 49. NN. Stan; 50. JJ. Albert.

Quiz 78
1. G. 2. E, N, O, V, Y. 3. U. 4. C, H, I, X. 5. M.
6. K. 7. J, AA. 8. D. 9. T. 10. V. 11. P, R. Z. 12.
F. 13. W. 14. A, L. 15. S. 16. Q. 17. B.

Quiz 80

Master Code Key (It's a backwards alphabet): A = Z; B = Y; C = X; D = W; E = V; F = U; G = T; H = S; I = R; J = Q; K = P; L = O; M = N; N = M; O = L; P = K; Q = J; R = I; S = H; T = G; U = F; V = E; W = D; X = C; Y = B; Z = A.

1. "Hi-yo Silver, AWAYYYYY!" (from *It*). 2. "I know what you need." (from "I Know What You Need"). 3. "Let's talk, you and I. Let's talk about fear." (from the Foreword to *Night Shift*). 4. "Do you love?" (from "Nona"). 5. "Redrum." (from *The Shining*). 6. "yerrrnnn umber whunnnn fayunnnn" (from *Misery*). 7. "They float." (from *It*). 8. "Shooting Stars Only." (from "The Langoliers"; *Four Past Midnight*). 9. "I'm king of the world!" (from "Apt Pupil"; *Different Seasons*). 10. "Sally." (from *The Stand: The Complete & Uncut Edition*).

Quiz 81

1. *The Tommyknockers*, B. 1987; 2. *Carrie*, J. 1974; 3. *Creepshow*, K. 1982; 4. *Firestarter*, L. 1980; 5. *Four Past Midnight*, F. 1990; 6. *Danse Macabre*, E. 1981; 7. *Needful Things*, O. 1991; 8. *Pet Sematary*, H. 1983; 9. *Night Shift*, G. 1978; 10. *'Salem's Lot*, N. 1975; 11. *It*, C. 1986; 12. *The Stand: The Complete & Uncut Edition*, F. 1990; 13. *The Shining*, D. 1977; 14. *The Talisman*, I. 1984; 15. *Skeleton Crew*, M. 1985; 16. *Misery*, B. 1987; 17. *The Dark Half*, A. 1989; 18. *The Eyes of the Dragon*, B. 1987; 19. *Christine*, H. 1983; 20. *Thinner*, I. 1984.

Quiz 82

1. A. 2. F. 3. D. 4. A. 5. E. 6. A. 7. D. 8. A. 9. E. 10. D. 11. B. 12. C. 13. F. 14. A. 15. B. 16. F. 17. D. 18. A. 19. D. 20. D. 21. F. 22. C. 23. A. 24. D. 25. A. 26. A. 27. B. 28. A. 29. D. 30. A. 31. C. 32. C. 33. D. 34. E. 35. D.

Quiz 83

1. Carrie White (*Carrie*). This was a poem Carrie turned in to her seventh grade English teacher, Mr. Edwin King, as a class assignment. The border of the paper on which this poem was written was "decorated with a great many cruciform figures which almost [seemed] to dance . . ." 2. Larry Underwood (*The Stand*). These are some of the lyrics to Larry's hit single "Baby, Can You Dig Your Man?" 3. Ben Hanscom (*It*). This was the haiku Ben wrote for Beverly. 4. Jim Gardener (*The Tommyknockers*). These are the opening lines from Jim's long poem, "Leighton Street," from his collection *Grimoire*. 5. Stephen King. These are the three kernel images King came up with in an early morning English class that evolved into the short story "The Blue Air Compressor." 6. Jake Chambers (*The Dark Tower III: The Waste Lands*). This was part of a song Jake had learned in summer camp at the age of seven or eight and which he sang in the sewers of Lud when commanded by Gasher to come up with something to keep the haunts away.

Quiz 84

1. Q, Bobbi Anderson, *The Tommyknockers* 2. F, Gordon Lachance, "The Body," *Different Seasons* 3. O, John Shooter, "Secret Window, Secret Garden," *Four Past Midnight* 4. P, Paul Sheldon, *Misery* 5. H, Bill Denbrough, *It* 6. J, Norma Watson, *Carrie* 7. I, Vic Trenton, *Cujo* 8. C, Jack Torrance, *The Shining* 9. A, Gerald Nately, "The Blue Air Compressor" 10. H, Bill Denbrough, *It* 11. B, Branson Buddinger, *It* 12. K, Alhazred, *The Eyes of the Dragon* 13. N, Susan Snell, *Carrie* 14. L, Larry Underwood, *The Stand* 15. P, Paul Sheldon, *Misery* 16. D, C. K. Summers, "The Jaunt," *Skeleton Crew* 17. M, George Stark, *The Dark Half* 18. G, Thad Beaumont & George Stark, *The Dark Half* 19. E, Mike Hanlon, *It* 20. P, Paul Sheldon, *Misery*

Quiz 85

1. Z. Charlie Gereson, "The Crate" (*Gallery* text version) 2. E. Mrs. Guilder, *Christine* 3. K. Edward Gray Seville, "The Breathing Method," *Different Seasons* 4. X. Dr. Emlyn McCarron, "The Breathing Method," *Different Seasons* 5. C. Bobbi Anderson, *The Tommyknockers* 6. V. Jack Torrance, *The Shining*. 7. A. Steve Kemp, *Cujo* 8. BB. David Drayton, "The Mist," *Skeleton Crew* 9. F. Rev. Lester Lowe, *Cycle of the Werewolf* 10. L. Jim Gardener, *The Tommyknockers* 11. Y. Thad Beaumont, *The Dark Half* 12. B. Ben Hanscom, *It* 13. S. John Kintner, "Secret Window, Secret Garden," *Four Past Midnight* 14. U. Robert Jenkins, "The Langoliers," *Four Past Midnight* 15. P. The Dead Beats, "Sneakers" 16. Q. Carlos Detweiller, *The Plant* 17. M. Peter Jefferies, "Dedication" 18. N. Morton Rainey, "Secret Window, Secret Garden," *Four Past Midnight* 19. R. John and Elise Graham, "Rainy Season" 20. M. Peter Jefferies, "Dedication" 21. T. Phyllis Myers, *The Dark Half* 22. I. George Stark, *The Dark Half* 23. C. Bobbi Anderson, *The Tommyknockers* 24. Y. Thad Beaumont, *The Dark Half* 25. J. Reg Thorpe, "The Ballad of the Flexible Bullet," *Skeleton Crew* 26. W. Larry Underwood, *The Stand* 27. H. Hank Olson, *The Long Walk* 28. G. Ben Mears, *'Salem's Lot* 29. AA. Gordon Lachance, "The Body," *Different Seasons* 30. O. Peter Rosewall, "Dedication"

Quiz 86

1. *Misery* 2. *'Salem's Lot* 3. *The Tommyknockers* 4. *The Dark Tower: The Gunslinger* 5. *Rage* 6. *The Stand* 7. *Cycle of the Werewolf* 8. "The Sun Dog" (*Four Past Midnight*) 9. *Danse Macabre* 10. "Rita Hayworth and Shawshank Redemption" (*Different Seasons*) 11. *The Shining* 12. *Christine* 13. *Skeleton Crew* 14. "Secret Window, Secret Garden" (*Four Past Midnight*) 15. *The Stand: The Complete & Uncut Edition* 16. *The Dark Half* 17. *The Talisman* 18. *Firestarter* 19. *Roadwork* 20. *Pet Sematary* 21. *The Dark Tower II: The*

Drawing of the Three 22. *The Dead Zone* 23. *The Eyes of the Dragon* 24. "The Langoliers" (*Four Past Midnight*) 25. "The Breathing Method" (*Different Seasons*) 26. *Carrie* 27. *It* 28. *The Long Walk* 29. "The Library Policeman" (*Four Past Midnight*) 30. "Apt Pupil" (*Different Seasons*)

Quiz 87
1. T. *The Plant* 2. U. "The Body," *Different Seasons* 3. D. *The Dark Half* 4. E. *It* 5. Y. *Pet Sematary* 6. P. *Thinner* 7. X. "The Mist," *Skeleton Crew* 8. AA. *The Running Man* 9. G. *Firestarter* 10. M. "The Breathing Method," *Different Seasons* 11. Z. *The Dead Zone* 12. J. *The Shining* 13. N. *'Salem's Lot* 14. K. *The Long Walk* 15. B. *Carrie* 16. I. *Christine* 17. K. *The Long Walk* 18. E. *It* 19. R. *The Tommyknockers* 20. F. *Cycle of the Werewolf* 21. E. *It* 22. A. *The Stand: The Complete & Uncut Edition* 23. C. *Misery* 24. W. *Four Past Midnight* 25. P. *Thinner* 16. O. *Talisman* 27. H. *Roadwork* 28. B. *Carrie* 29. V. "Before the Play" 30. R. *The Tommyknockers* 31. Q. *The Dark Tower II: The Drawing of the Three* 32. S. "The Library Policeman," *Four Past Midnight* 33. D. *The Dark Half* 34. C. *Misery* 35. Q. *The Dark Tower II: The Drawing of the Three* 36. E. *It* 37. F. *Cycle of the Werewolf* 38. S. "The Library Policeman," *Four Past Midnight* 39. D. *The Dark Half* 40. J. *The Shining* 41. O. *The Talisman* 42. J. *The Shining* 43. Z. *The Dead Zone* 44. G. *Firestarter* 45. H. *Roadwork* 46. N. *'Salem's Lot* 47. J. *The Shining* 48. A. *The Stand: The Complete & Uncut Edition* 49. I. *Christine* 50. L. *The Stand*

Quiz 88
1. B, Donald M. Grant, Publisher (1983) 2. A, Edition Phantasia (1986) 3. J, Land of Enchantment (1983) 4. C, Philtrum Press (1984) 5. C, Philtrum Press (1982, 1983, 1985) 6. H, Mysterious Press (1981) 7. B, Donald M. Grant, Publisher (1987) 8. I, Everest House (1981) 9. G, Lord John Press (1989) 10. F, Scream Press (1985) 11. D, Doubleday (1990) 12. E,

Whitney Museum of American Art (1989) 13. B, Donald M. Grant, Publisher (1984) 14. K, Phantasia Press (1980) 15. B, Donald M. Grant, Publisher (1982)
The Truly "No Limits" Bonus Section 1. C, Underwood-Miller (1986) 2. A, The Overlook Connection Press (1991) 3. B, GB Publishing (1989) 4. C, Underwood-Miller (1988) 5. B, GB Publishing (1991)

Quiz 89
1. E, *Rage* 2. D, "The Woman in the Room" 3. A, *The Shining* 4. B, "Sometimes They Come Back" 5. C, *'Salem's Lot*

Quiz 90
1. A. 2. N. 3. E. 4. F. 5. C. 6. V. 7. M. 8. J. 9. AA. 10. W. 11. O. 12. U. 13. X. 14. Z. 15. Q. 16. K. 17. L. 18. Y. 19. DD. 20. S. 21. P. 22. H. 23. T. 24. BB. 25. I. 26. D. 27. B. 28. G. 29. CC. 30. R.

Quiz 91
1. E, N. 2. M. 3. F. 4. G. 5. I. 6. C. 7. D. 8. F. 9. H. 10. E. 11. A. 12. K. 13. B. 14. J. 15. R. 16. F. 17. O. 18. Q, S, T. 19. P. 20. N.

Quiz 92
1. G; 2. E; 3. I; 4. H; 5. F; 6. J; 7. C; 8. D; 9. A; 10. B.

Quiz 93
1. "Doc." 2. Lard Ass." 3. "Shitters." 4. "Dirty Birds" or "Dirty Birdies." 5. A "lunkhead." 6. "The mangler." 7. "Tony." 8. "The Losers' Club." 9. "The Monster Words." 10. "Bears."

Quiz 94
1. G. Jack *Daniel* Torrance 2. D. Danny *Anthony* Torrance 3. H. Greg *Ammas* Stillson 4. F. Glen *Pequod* Bateman 5. A. Morgan *Luther* Sloat 6. L. Donald *Merwin* Elbert 7. C. Johnny *no middle name* Smith 8. J. Harold *Emery* Lauder 9. I. George *Elmer*

Denbrough 10. K. Hubert *Barclay* Marsten 11. Ray *Paul* Rexer 12. Stephen *Edwin* King

Quiz 95

A. They are all male characters with the initials "R. F"; the same as Randall Flagg.

B. Criterion A is "Good"; Criterion B is "Evil." The two lists are:

"A": *GOOD*	"B": *EVIL*
Roger Fearon	Randall Flagg
Richard Farris	Ramsey Forrest
Ray Flowers	Robert Franq
Roger Fenum	Richard Fry
Roscoe Fisher	Russell Faraday
Rand Foxworth	Richard Freemantle
Ron Frane	Robert Freemont
Raymond Fogarty	Richard Frye
Ralph Foster	Richard Folsom
Russ Frame	Rudy Foggia
Robert Farnham	Richard Fannin
Richard Fornoy	

C. The "Evil" list consists *only* of Randall Flagg (and all his manifestations) and two *other* characters that are obviously Mr. X and Mr. Y. Mr. X is Richard Folsom, and Mr. Y is Rudy Foggia.

D. From the fact that every other "R. F." character in Stephen King's work is a good guy *except* for Richard Folsom and Rudy Foggia, it would be fair to surmise that Richard Folsom was a manifestation of Flagg who worked for The Shop, and that in the year 2037 (the year in which "The Jaunt" takes place), Rudy Foggia is probably a future manifestation of Randall Flagg.

Quiz 96

1. F, "The Blue Air Compressor" 2. E, "The Night Flier" 3. G, *Thinner* 4. A, *Carrie* 5. C, *The Stand* 6. D, *It* 7. B, "The Library Policeman"

A Stephen King Bibliography

Part One: Novels and Collections

This bibliography is in two parts: *Novels and Collections*, and *Short Stories and Novellas*. (This is an updated version of the bibliography that appeared in *The Stephen King Quiz Book*.)

For the novels and collections, I've listed those editions of the works that I felt were the most accessible and would be the easiest to find. I've omitted the limited editions, since you're probably not going to go out and spend hundreds of dollars for *The Drawing of the Three* when the NAL trade paperback can be had for $10.95. Following this line of reasoning, I also omitted bibliographic information for the original Signet editions of Richard Bachman's novels. These are now collector's items, and are priced accordingly. All you need to answer the quiz questions is the NAL paperback edition of these novels, and so these mass-market volumes are the books I chose to include here.

The Short Story and Novellas bibliography is not the complete listing of Stephen King's shorter works. It consists of the works included in *The Stephen King Quiz Book* and *The Second Stephen King Quiz Book* as quiz subjects (or stories referred to in the book), and it lists, once again, what I felt were the easiest to find.

When trying to track down these tales, don't overlook your local public library. Many of the anthologies listed are available in libraries, and if your local library doesn't have it, it's likely that they can get a copy of the book through an inter-library loan. Used bookstores are often a gold mine for this kind of stuff and should not be overlooked either.

Also, keep in mind the mail-order companies listed in the "sources" section of the bibliography. Many of these dealers have very complete "Stephen King" inventories that they will be more than happy to part with. Get on their mailing lists and check out their catalogs. They will more than likely have what you are looking for.

• *The Bachman Books*
Hardcover: New York: New American Library, NAL Books, 1985.
Trade paperback: New York: New American Library, Plume, 1985.
Paperback: New York: New American Library, Signet, 1986.

• *Carrie*
Hardcover: Garden City, NY: Doubleday, 1974.
Trade paperback: New York: New American Library, Plume, 1991 (Collectors Edition)
Paperback: New York: New American Library, Signet, 1975.

• *Christine*
Hardcover: New York: Viking, 1983.
Paperback: New York: New American Library, Signet, 1984.

• *Creepshow*
Trade paperback: New York: New American Library, Plume, 1982.

• *Cujo*
Hardcover: New York: Viking, 1981.
Paperback: New York: New American Library, Signet, 1982.

- *Cycle of the Werewolf*
  Trade paperback: New York: New American Library, Plume, 1985.

- *The Dark Half* (with Richard Bachman)
  Hardcover: New York: Viking, 1989.
  Paperback: New York: New American Library, Signet, 1990.

- *The Dark Tower: The Gunslinger*
  Trade paperback: New York: New American Library, Plume, 1988.

- *The Dark Tower II: The Drawing of the Three*
  Trade paperback: New York: New American Library, Plume, 1989.

- *The Dark Tower III: The Waste Lands*
  Trade paperback: New York: New American Library, Plume, 1991.

- *The Dead Zone*
  Hardcover: New York: Viking, 1979.
  Paperback: New York: New American Library, Signet, 1980.

- *Different Seasons*
  Hardcover: New York: Viking, 1982.
  Paperback: New York: New American Library, Signet, 1983.

- *The Eyes of the Dragon*
  Hardcover: New York: Viking, 1987.
  Paperback: New York: New American Library, Signet, 1988.

- *Firestarter*
  Hardcover: New York: Viking, 1980.
  Paperback: New York: New American Library, Signet, 1981.

- *Four Past Midnight*
   Hardcover: New York: Viking, 1990.
   Paperback: New York: New American Library, Signet, 1991.

- *It*
   Hardcover: New York: Viking, 1986.
   Paperback: New York: New American Library, Signet, 1987.

- *The Long Walk* (in *The Bachman Books*)
   Trade paperback: New York: New American Library, Plume, 1985.
   Paperback: New York: New American Library, Signet, 1986.

- *Misery*
   Hardcover: New York: Viking, 1987.
   Paperback: New York: New American Library, Signet, 1988.

- *Needful Things*
   Hardcover: New York: Viking, 1991.
   Paperback: New York: New American Library, Signet, 1992.

- *Night Shift*
   Hardcover: Garden City, NY: Doubleday, 1978.
   Paperback: New York: New American Library, Signet, 1979.

- *Pet Sematary*
   Hardcover: Garden City, NY: Doubleday, 1983.
   Paperback: New York: New American Library, Signet, 1984.

- *Rage* (in *The Bachman Books*)
   Trade paperback: New York: New American Library, Plume, 1985.

Paperback: New York: New American Library, Signet, 1986.

• *Roadwork* (in *The Bachman Books*)
Trade paperback: New York: New American Library, Plume, 1985.
Paperback: New York: New American Library, Signet, 1986.

• *The Running Man* (in *The Bachman Books*)
Trade paperback: New York: New American Library, Plume, 1985.
Paperback: New York: New American Library, Signet, 1986.

• *'Salem's Lot*
Hardcover: Garden City, NY: Doubleday, 1975.
Trade paperback: New York: New American Library, Plume, 1991 (Collectors Edition)
Paperback: New York: New American Library, Signet, 1976.

• *The Shining*
Hardcover: Garden City, NY: Doubleday, 1977.
Trade paperback: New York: New American Library, Plume, 1991 (Collectors Edition)
Paperback: New York: New American Library, Signet, 1978.

• *Skeleton Crew*
Hardcover: New York: Putnam, 1985.
Paperback: New York: New American Library, Signet, 1986.

• *The Stand*
Hardcover: Garden City, NY: Doubleday, 1978.
Paperback: New York: New American Library, Signet, 1979.

- *The Stand: The Complete & Uncut Edition*
  Hardcover: Garden City, NY: Doubleday, 1990.
  Paperback: New York: New American Library, Signet, 1991.

- *The Talisman* (with Peter Straub)
  Hardcover: New York: Viking and Putnam, 1984.
  Paperback: New York: Berkley, 1985.

- *Thinner* (as Richard Bachman)
  Hardcover: New York: New American Library, NAL Books, 1984.
  Paperback: New York: New American Library, Signet, 1985.

- *The Tommyknockers*
  Hardcover: New York: Putnam, 1987.
  Paperback: New York: New American Library, Signet, 1988

Part Two: Short Stories and Novellas

- "Apt Pupil"
  Different Seasons, 1982.

- "The Ballad of the Flexible Bullet"
  Skeleton Crew, 1985.

- "Battleground"
  Night Shift, 1978.

- "Beachworld"
  Skeleton Crew, 1985.

- "Before the Play"
  1. *Whispers*, August 1982.

- "Big Wheels: A Tale of the Laundry Game (Milkman #2)"
  Skeleton Crew, 1985.

- "The Body"
  Different Seasons, 1982.

- "The Boogeyman"
  Night Shift, 1978.

- "The Breathing Method"
  Different Seasons, 1982.

- "Cain Rose Up"
  Skeleton Crew, 1985.

- "The Cat From Hell"
  1. *Cavalier*, June 1977.
  2. *The Year's Finest Fantasy*. Ed. Terry Carr (Berkley paperback, 1979).
  3. *Magicats!* Ed. Jack Dann and Gardner Dozois (Ace paperback, 1984).

- "Children of the Corn"
  Night Shift, 1978.

- "The Crate"
  Creepshow, 1982.

- "Crouch End"
  1. *New Tales of the Cthulhu Mythos*. Ed. Ramsey Campbell (Arkham House hardcover, 1980)
  2. *The Dark Descent*. Ed. David G. Hartwell (Tor hardcover, 1987).

- "Dedication"
  Night Visions 5. Ed. Douglas E. Winter (Dark Harvest, 1988).

- "The Doctor's Case"
  The New Adventures of Sherlock Holmes. Ed. Martin Harry Greenberg and Carol-Lynn Rössel Waugh (Carroll & Graf hardcover, 1987).

- "Dolan's Cadillac"
  1. *Castle Rock: The Stephen King Newsletter*, February–June 1985.
  2. (Lord John Press edition, 1988).

- "Father's Day"
  Creepshow, 1982.

- "The Fifth Quarter"
  1. *Cavalier*, April 1972. (Written as John Swithen).
  2. *Twilight Zone Magazine*, February 1986. (Reprinted as by Stephen King.)

- "For the Birds"
  1. *Bred Any Good Rooks Lately?* Ed. James Charlton (Doubleday trade paperback, 1986).

- "The Glass Floor"
  1. *Startling Mystery Stories*. (Fall 1967).
  2. *Weird Tales*. (Fall 1990).

- "Gramma"
  Skeleton Crew, 1985.

- "Graveyard Shift"
  Night Shift, 1978.

- "Gray Matter"
  Night Shift, 1978.

- "The Gunslinger and the Dark Man"
  The Dark Tower: The Gunslinger (Plume, 1988).

- "The Gunslinger"
  The Dark Tower: The Gunslinger (Plume, 1988).

- "Here There Be Tygers"
  Skeleton Crew, 1985.

- "Home Delivery"
  The Book of the Dead (Bantam paperback, 1989).

- "I Am the Doorway"
  Night Shift, 1978.

- "I Know What You Need"
  Night Shift, 1978.

- "The Jaunt"
  Skeleton Crew, 1985.

- "Jerusalem's Lot"
  Night Shift, 1978.

- "The Last Rung on the Ladder"
  Night Shift, 1978.

- "The Lawnmower Man"
  Night Shift, 1978.

- "The Ledge"
  Night Shift, 1978.

- "The Lonesome Death of Jordy Verrill"
  Creepshow, 1982.

- "The Man Who Loved Flowers"
  Night Shift, 1978.

- "The Man Who Would Not Shake Hands"
  Skeleton Crew, 1985.

- "The Mangler"
  Night Shift, 1978.

- "The Mist"
  Skeleton Crew, 1985.

- "The Monkey"
  Skeleton Crew, 1985.

- "Morning Deliveries (Milkman #1)"
  Skeleton Crew, 1985.

- "The Moving Finger"
  1. *The Magazine of Fantasy & Science Fiction*, December 1990

- "Mrs. Todd's Shortcut"
  Skeleton Crew, 1985.

- "My Pretty Pony"
  My Pretty Pony (Alfred A. Knopf hardcover, 1989).

- "The Night Flier"
  Prime Evil. Ed. Douglas E. Winter (New American Library, NAL Books hardcover, 1988; NAL/Signet paperback, 1989).

- "The Night of the Tiger"
  1. *The Magazine of Fantasy and Science Fiction*, February 1978.
  2. *The Year's Best Horror Stories VII* (Daw paperback, 1978).
  3. *The Best Horror Stories from the Magazine of Fantasy and Science Fiction* (Simon and Schuster paperback, 1989)

- "Night Surf"
  Night Shift, 1978.

- "Nona"
  Skeleton Crew, 1985.

- "One for the Road"
  Night Shift, 1978.

- "The Oracle and the Mountains"
  The Dark Tower: The Gunslinger (Plume, 1988).

- "Popsy"
  Masques II. Ed. J. N. Williamson (Maclay hardcover, 1987).
  Best of Masques. Ed. J. N. Williamson (Berkley paperback, 1988).

- "Quitters, Inc."
  Night Shift, 1978.

- "The Raft"
  Skeleton Crew, 1985.

- "Rainy Season"
  Midnight Graffiti, Spring 1989.

- "The Reach"
  Skeleton Crew, 1985.

- "The Reaper's Image"
  Skeleton Crew, 1985.

- "The Reploids"
  Night Visions 5. Ed. Douglas E. Winter (Dark Harvest, 1988).

- "Rita Hayworth and Shawshank Redemption"
  Different Seasons, 1982.

- "The Slow Mutants"
  The Dark Tower: The Gunslinger (Plume, 1988).

- "Sneakers"
  Night Visions 5. Ed. Douglas E. Winter (Dark Harvest, 1988).

- "Something to Tide You Over"
  Creepshow, 1982.

- "Sometimes They Come Back"
  Night Shift, 1978.

- "Strawberry Spring"
  Night Shift, 1978.

- "Suffer the Little Children"
  1. *Cavalier*, February 1972.
  2. *Nightmares*. Ed. Charles L. Grant (Playboy paperback, 1979).
  3. *The Evil Image: Two Centuries of Gothic Short Fiction and Poetry*. Eds. Patricia L. Skarda and Nora Crow Jaffe (New American Library, Meridian, 1981).

- "Survivor Type"
  Skeleton Crew, 1985.

- "They're Creeping Up On You"
  Creepshow, 1982.

- "Trucks"
  Night Shift, 1978.

- "Uncle Otto's Truck"
  Skeleton Crew, 1985.

- "The Way Station"
  The Dark Tower: The Gunslinger (Plume, 1988).

- "The Wedding Gig"
  Skeleton Crew, 1985.

- "The Woman in the Room"
  Night Shift, 1978.

- "Word Processor of the Gods"
  Skeleton Crew, 1985.

- "You Know They Got a Hell of a Band"
  Shock Rock. Ed. Jeff Gelb (Pocket Books paperback, 1992).

Other Books of Interest

• *Danse Macabre* by Stephen King.
Paperback: New York: Berkley, 1983.

Incredible. Stephen King, in his only book-length work of nonfiction, takes an unblinking look at the horror field through 1980, and the reader comes away openmouthed with amazement. A very valuable contribution to the genre. *Danse Macabre* makes you wish King would decide to do Volume 2, in which he took a look at the field from 1980 through 1990. I, for one, would love to know his thoughts about the past decade's genre novels, films, magazines, and TV programs.

• *Stephen King: The Art of Darkness* by Douglas E. Winter.
Paperback: New York: New American Library, Signet, 1986.

A fantastic book that looks at King's life and fiction. Winter is a superb critic—he knows of what he speaks, and his in-depth interpretations of King's novels, themes, subtexts, and style will enlighten and educate you. For any serious King fan, *The Art of Darkness* is must-reading.

• *The Shape Under the Sheet: The Complete Stephen King Encyclopedia* by Stephen J. Spignesi.
Hardcover: Ann Arbor, MI: Popular Culture, Ink., 1991.

Just what the title says: An exhaustive 750,000 word encyclopedia covering every person, place, and thing in King's fiction. The 18,000 entry annotated concordance will help you with many of the questions in both *Stephen King Quiz Books*. *The Shape Under the Sheet* also contains mountains of other information, including interviews, photos, and essays on King, his work, and the entire King Phenomenon.

- *The Stephen King Companion* by George Beahm
Trade paperback: Kansas City, MO: Andrews and McMeel, 1989.

The *perfect* introductory volume to King and his world. Loaded with articles, interviews, photos, and sidebars, the *Companion* gives the novice King much-needed information in one compact, nicely designed volume. The address section and the bibliography are extremely helpful, and after a journey through *The Stephen King Companion*, the reader emerges a more seasoned traveler in the (sometimes daunting) land of King.

- *The Stephen King Story* by George Beahm
Hardcover: Kansas City, MO: Andrews and McMeel, 1991.

A comprehensive, appreciative biography that wisely focuses on the "making of a writer," rather than the type of exploitation so commonly seen today. Beahm is a meticulous researcher who is very careful with his presentation of facts. He is also an insightful biographer, and you come away from *The Stephen King Story* with a better sense of where all those stories *come from*. A necessary book written by a scholar who also happens to be a fan.

- *Bare Bones*. Ed. by Tim Underwood and Chuck Miller.
Hardcover: New York: McGraw-Hill, 1988.

Huge collection of more than two dozen interviews with King, ranging from 1979 through 1985. They're all reprints, but the book is a very valuable resource nonetheless. Many of the interviews included here are now out of print and thus, very difficult to find. It's good to have them all in one volume.

- *Dark Dreamers: Conversations with the Masters of Horror* by Stanley Wiater.
Trade Paperback: New York: Avon Books, 1990.

A superlative collection of interviews with the masters in the field, including Stephen King, Peter Straub, Richard Matheson, Dean Koontz, Robert Bloch, Clive Barker, and twenty others. Stanley Wiater is an accomplished interviewer and writer and the interviews are insightful, informative, and *very* entertaining. *Dark Dreamers* (and its companion volume *Dark Visions*) is a must for horror and dark fantasy fans.

• *Dark Visions: Conversations with the Masters of the Horror Film* by Stanley Wiater.
Trade Paperback: New York: Avon Books, 1992.
Another terrific collection of interviews by Stanley Wiater, this time with the luminaries in the field of horror film directing. This volume functions as an overview of the contemporary horror film industry, and contains nearly two dozen interviews with a variety of talents. Included are talks with directors David Cronenberg, George Romero, and John Carpenter; actors Vincent Price and Robert Englund; screenwriters Michael McDowell and Joseph Stefano; as well as special effects masters such as Stan Winston and Kevin Yagher. Several of Stephen King's film adaptations are discussed in detail.

• *The Shorter Works of Stephen King* by Michael R. Collings and David Engebretson.
Paperback: Mercer Island, WA: Starmont House, 1985.
An excellent companion to King's shorter work. Good sections on the rare, uncollected materials, too.

• *The Unseen King* by Tyson Blue.
Paperback: Mercer Island, WA: Starmont House, 1985.
This is an excellent introduction to King's rare and uncollected stories. Tyson Blue (like Doug Winter, George Beahm, Michael Collings, and my-

self) has spent more time reading and studying Stephen King's works than any normal person walking the streets a free man probably should. The result is an excellent, well-researched book.

• *Horror: 100 Best Books*, edited by Stephen Jones and Kim Newman
Trade paperback: New York: Carroll & Graf Publishers, 1988.

In this ambitious and clever undertaking, editors Jones and Newman assembled 100 of the most well-known writers in horror (including Stephen King, Clive Barker, Ramsey Campbell, Harlan Ellison, and others) and asked them to write about the 100 best books in the horror genre. The result is King writing about Robert Marasco's *Burnt Offerings*; Peter Straub writing about King's *The Shining*; F. Paul Wilson writing about William Peter Blatty's *The Exorcist*; Richard Christian Matheson writing about his father Richard Matheson's classic *I Am Legend*; and ninety-six other writers "reviewing" the greatest books in the field. A very informative and enlightening anthology that will greatly enhance your appreciation and understanding of the field. (It will also turn you on to some books you haven't—but should have—read. Guaranteed.)

• *The Penguin Encyclopedia of Horror and the Supernatural*, edited by Jack Sullivan
Trade hardcover: New York: Viking, 1986.

This is the best single-volume overview of the entire horror field to date. Arranged alphabetically, this encyclopedia lives up to its name and covers everything from the film *The Abominable Dr. Phibes* to "Zombies." The list of contributors reads like a "Who's Who" of horror literature and film. Everyone seems to be here: T.E.D. Klein, Kim Newman, Ramsey Campbell, John Crowley, Gary Crawford, Thomas M. Disch, Leslie Fiedler, Ron Goulart, Darrell Schweitzer, Michele Slung, Whitley Strieber, Colin Wilson, and Douglas Winter are among the writers who participated in this monumental effort. In addition to the alphabetical "dictionary" style look at horror, there are also comprehensive and insightful essays scattered throughout the volume on subjects such as "B Movies," "Ghosts," "Graveyard Poetry," "Opera," "Sex," "Small Press Magazines," "Television," "Urban and Pastoral Horror," and forty-six other related topics. This is a superior effort that will serve you well over decades of use.

ALSO . . .
• *Discovering Stephen King*, edited by Darrell Schweitzer.
• *Stephen King as Richard Bachman* by Michael R. Collings.
• *The Many Facets of Stephen King* by Michael R. Collings.
• *The Films of Stephen King* by Michael R. Collings.
• *The Stephen King Phenomenon* by Michael R. Collings.
• *The Moral Voyages of Stephen King* by Anthony Magistrale.
• The Shining *Reader* by Anthony Magistrale.
• *Infinite Explorations: Art and Artifice in Stephen King's* It, Misery, *and* The Tommyknockers by Michael R. Collings.
• *Notes from the Terminator: Thoughts of Stephen King and Other Horrorists* by Tyson Blue.
(All of the above are available in paperback from Starmont House.)

• *Stephen King at the Movies* by Jessie Horsting. (NAL/Signet trade paperback, 1986.) A very informative, and *very* entertaining look at the film versions of King's stories. Recommended.

Addresses of Sources:

•POPULAR CULTURE, INK., PUBLISHERS
 P.O. Box 1839
 Ann Arbor, MI 48106
 (Phone: 1-800-678-8828)

The publishers of *The Shape Under the Sheet: The Complete Stephen King Encyclopedia* by Stephen J. Spignesi, and many other volumes of interest for popular culture aficionados. (Like books about "The Andy Griffith Show," The Beatles [twenty at last count], Bob Dylan, Hot Rod Music, Chuck Berry, Elvis, Michael Jackson, The Rolling Stones, the "Psychedelic Sixties," and George Gershwin, just to name a few.) For serious fans of any of these subjects, Tom Schultheiss's and Pat Curtis's Popular Culture, Ink. is the ultimate source for books that give new meaning to the word *thorough*. Write or call for a catalog.

•THE OVERLOOK CONNECTION
 P.O. Box 526
 Woodstock, GA 30188
 (Phone/Fax: 404-926-1762; Monday–Friday, 7:00 P.M. to Midnight)
 Distribution Center: Phone/Fax: 704-837-8089; Monday–Friday, Noon to 5 P.M. (Ask for Steve Chamberlain.)

Great source for hard-to-find anthologies, first editions, and magazine appearances in horror, science fiction, fantasy, and mystery. Jam-packed magazine-style catalog loaded with everything from fiction to photos. Dave Hinchberger is the hotel manager and still as off-the-wall as ever. You'll love Dave and the Overlook. (Dave and his fetching wife Laurie recently founded The Overlook Connection Press, a publishing arm of the Overlook Connection. Their first release was the limited edition of my own *Shape Under the Sheet*. Their 1992 release was the hardcover edition of Gary Raisor's first novel, *Less Than Human*, a chilling modern vampire tale. Get on The Overlook's mailing list for news of future releases, as well as catalogs.)

•TIME TUNNEL
313 Beechwood Avenue
Middlesex, NJ 08846
(Phone: 908-560-0738)

Craig Goden's *Time Tunnel* is another excellent source of Stephen King-related items. (Craig was my source for King's 1970 anti-war essay "A Possible Fairy Tale" detailed in my *Shape Under the Sheet*.) They issue a very comprehensive "newsletter"-type catalog, and their magazine inventory is wide-ranging and complete. *Time Tunnel* stocks many of the harder-to-find items, everyone there is extremely helpful, and I wholeheartedly recommend them to you for your genre needs. Craig Goden is one of the most informed guys in the business, and he can usually answer any question you throw at him. Get on their mailing list.

• STARMONT HOUSE PUBLISHERS
P.O. Box 851
Mercer Island, WA 98040

The publishers of several volumes about King and his work. For books of critique and in-depth interpretive analysis of genre fiction (including, of course, the work of Stephen King), you can't get any better than the offerings from Starmont. Write for a catalog.

Magazines of Interest

• *Midnight Graffiti*
13101 Sudan Road
Poway, CA 92064

Excellent—and important—dark fantasy quarterly. Their third issue was a Stephen King special, and it contained the first appearance of the King short story "Rainy Season," as well as an excerpt from *The Shape Under the Sheet*. Now with the demise of *Twilight Zone Magazine*, *Midnight Graffiti* is one of only a handful of sources left for state-of-the-art horror and dark fantasy short fiction and information. The mag is hard to find on newsstands, so if you don't want to miss out, SUBSCRIBE! Stephen King reads *Midnight Graffiti*. Shouldn't you?

• *Cinefantastique*
P.O. Box 270
Oak Park, IL 60303

Cinefantastique is without a doubt the best magazine ever for in-depth coverage of horror, science fiction, and fantasy films. Their February 1991 issue was a special "Stephen King" issue and featured no less than twenty-two articles and features on King and the film versions of his work (including a biographical piece on King adapted from my own *Shape Under the Sheet*). The magazine itself is absolutely gorgeous: they use glossy paper, color photos, and a very appealing graphic design. *CFQ* is must-reading for genre film buffs.

• *Gauntlet: Exploring the Limits of Free Expression*
309 Powell Road
Springfield, PA 19064

Barry Hoffman's *Gauntlet* is an annual publication that publishes censored material and serves as a forum for the discussion of topics having to do with free speech in America. I have been known to call *Gauntlet* the "most important magazine being published today," and I stand by that assertion. The censors are everywhere, and Barry Hoffman does a brilliant job of shining a light on the dark, slimy corners where they hide, and from which they spit out their "holier-than-thou, we know better" bullshit. But don't get me wrong: the magazine is not all tirade! The second issue of *Gauntlet* was a special "Stephen King" issue and featured a lengthy piece by King on the movie rating system. *Gauntlet* also publishes fiction, artwork, and interviews, and is well worth your time (and financial support.)

• *Cemetery Dance*
P.O. Box 16372
Baltimore, MD 21210

Stephen King calls *Cemetery Dance* "one of the best," and he is right. This is as close to a general interest horror genre magazine as you're going to find. The mag has columns with up-to-date info (including a "Stephen King" news column called "Needful Kings" by Tyson Blue), book reviews, interviews, and, of course, fiction. Richard Chizmar and his wife Kara Tipton do a masterful job of putting out a terrific periodical.

• *The Magazine of Fantasy & Science Fiction*
Box 56
Cornwall, CT 06753
This is one of the granddaddies of genre magazines. They have been publishing continuously for decades, and have consistently offered some of the finest science fiction and horror fiction from the world's best writers. (Harlan Ellison writes their film review column, and that should give you an idea of the caliber of writing they routinely publish. His film columns were recently collected in a massive volume called *Harlan Ellison's Watching* that is must-reading for horror and science fiction film aficionados.) The December 1990 issue of *The Magazine of Fantasy & Science Fiction* featured a brand-new Stephen King short story, "The Moving Finger," and also presented the opening segment from the then still-unpublished *The Dark Tower III: The Waste Lands*. A very important magazine, and one well worth your time and money.

• *Weird Tales*®
P.O. Box 13418
Philadelphia, PA 19101
Weird Tales® bills themselves as "The Unique Magazine," and in this case, the billing is true. The magazine is a quarterly, and they publish a lot of fiction, as well as poetry, book reviews, and interviews in each issue. The Fall 1990 issue offered the first reprinting of Stephen King's first professional sale, "The Glass Floor," with a new introduction by King. *Weird*

Tales® is a significant source for important genre fiction. (The only thing about the magazine that annoys me is the little "®" that they put after *every* mention of the magazine's name. I *know* it's a registered trade name, but it does get to be a nuisance after a while.)

• *Deathrealm*
3223-F Regents Park Lane
Greensboro, NC 27405
(Phone: 919-288-9138)

Mark Rainey's *Deathrealm* began in 1987 and is a quarterly publication specializing in horror and dark fantasy. They bill themselves as "The Land Where Horror Dwells" and the material they publish is of superior quality. (Contributors have included Joe R. Lansdale, Elizabeth Massie, Allen Koszowski, and many others.) Like other genre publications, *Deathrealm* offers book and magazine reviews, interviews, fiction, and artwork. But to their credit, they also run dark fantasy and horror poetry in every issue, a welcome addition and a feature that adds a broader dimension to the magazine. As of issue #15, they were in 8 ½ × 11 format, with a cover price of $4.00. *Deathrealm* was awarded Best Magazine of 1990 by the Small Press Writers and Artists Organization, and they well deserved it.

• *Grue*
P.O. Box 370
Times Square Station
New York, NY 10108-0370
(Phone: 212-245-2329)

Grue publishes material they describe as "the raw edge of horror," and editor Peggy Nadramia told me she considers *Grue* the place "where tomorrow's Stephen Kings are presently cutting their teeth." *Grue* publishes state-of-the-art horror fiction: graphic, visceral, and, yes, raw. The magazine concentrates on fiction, poetry, and artwork, and offers material that is gripping and unique; thought-provoking and dark.

Grue is handsomely designed in an 8 ¼ × 5 ½ format and sells for $4.50 a copy. I can honestly say that I have read stories in *Grue* that have horrified and surprised me . . . and to tell the truth, that ain't an easy task! *Grue* received the 1990 World Fantasy Award, and stories from the mag's pages have appeared in several prestigious anthologies. If you like daring, explicit horror and dark fantasy fiction, you should definitely take a look at an issue of *Grue*.

About the Author

Stephen Spignesi is the author of three books about Stephen King: *The Stephen King Quiz Book* (NAL/Signet), *The Shape Under the Sheet: The Complete Stephen King Encyclopedia* (Popular Culture, Ink.), and *The Second Stephen King Quiz Book* (NAL/Signet). His first book was the "Andy Griffith Show" encyclopedia, *Mayberry, My Hometown* (Popular Culture, Ink.), which was recently released in paperback.

Steve's next book is *The Woody Allen Companion*, to be published in the fall of 1992 by Andrews and McMeel.

Steve lives in New Haven, Connecticut, with his wife Pam and their cat Ben. Pam is certain she has identified arcane Stephen King and Woody Allen references in the television show "Northern Exposure."

Steve's favorite Beatle was John Lennon and he's sure you all know why.